AI-Powered Grant Writing:
The Ultimate Guide to Secure More Funding with Artificial Intelligence

Anthony J Fitzpatrick Ed.D.

Copyright © 2025 Inedvation

All rights reserved.

No part of this book may be reproduced or transmitted in any form or by any means, electronic or mechanical, including photocopying, recording, or by any information storage and retrieval system, without permission in writing from the publisher.

ISBN-13: 978-0-9864377-4-8
Published in the United States of America
Inedvation

Dedication

To the grant writers, educators, nonprofit leaders, and changemakers who dedicate themselves to securing the resources needed to transform lives and strengthen communities—this book is for you.

To those who have spent countless late nights crafting proposals, refining budgets, and aligning their visions with funder priorities, may AI empower you, not replace you—enhancing your creativity, streamlining your process, and amplifying your impact.

To my mentors, colleagues, and peers who have inspired me with their passion for education, innovation, and funding equity—your dedication fuels the progress that makes a lasting difference.

To my family—your unwavering support and encouragement have been the foundation of every success.

And finally, to those who dare to embrace the future, who see AI not as a challenge but as an opportunity to revolutionize the way we fund meaningful work—this is just the beginning. 🚀

Contents

Dedication 3

Chapter 1: Understanding Grants and Funding Sources 21

Section 1: The Importance of Grants Across Industries 21

Why Grants Matter 21

The Challenges of Grant Writing 22

How AI is Transforming the Grant Writing Process 22

    Case Study: How AI Helped a School District Secure a STEM Grant 22

Practical AI Prompt Examples for Grant Writing 23

    1. Finding Grant Opportunities 23

    2. Generating a Problem Statement 23

    3. Drafting Key Proposal Sections 23

    4. Budget Justification Assistance 23

    5. Refining Language for Clarity 24

Looking Ahead 24

    Reflection Questions: 24

Section 2: Types of Grants and Their Funding Sources 24

Types of Grants 25

How to Identify the Right Type of Grant for Your Project 25

Case Study: How AI Helped a Nonprofit Find the Perfect Grant 26

Practical AI Prompts for Identifying Grants 26

    1. Finding Government Grants 26

    2. Searching for Foundation Grants 26

    3. Identifying Corporate Grants 26

    4. Matching Grants to Organizational Needs 27

    5. Generating a Summary of Grant Requirements 27

Looking Ahead 27

    Reflection Questions: 27

Section 3: The Structure of a Strong Grant Proposal 27

Key Components of a Grant Proposal 28

Common Pitfalls and How to Avoid Them 29

Case Study: How AI Helped a Small Business Write a Winning Proposal 29
Practical AI Prompts for Crafting a Strong Grant Proposal 30
- 1. Drafting a Persuasive Problem Statement 30
- 2. Structuring Project Goals and Objectives 30
- 3. Generating a Timeline for Implementation 30
- 4. Enhancing Budget Justifications 30
- 5. Editing and Refining for Clarity 30

Looking Ahead 30
- Reflection Questions: 31

Section 4: The Role of Data and Research in Grants 31
Why Data is Essential in Grant Writing 31
Types of Data to Include in Grant Proposals 32
How AI Enhances Data Collection and Analysis 33
Case Study: AI-Powered Data Analysis for an Educational Grant Proposal .. 33
Practical AI Prompts for Data-Driven Grant Writing 34
- 1. Finding Relevant Statistics 34
- 2. Summarizing Research Studies 34
- 3. Analyzing Trends and Patterns 34
- 4. Generating Data Visualizations 34
- 5. Crafting a Data-Backed Problem Statement 34

Looking Ahead 34
- Reflection Questions: 35

Section 5: Common Grant Writing Mistakes and How to Avoid Them   35
Top 5 Common Grant Writing Mistakes and Solutions 36
Case Study: How AI Helped Fix a Failing Grant Proposal 36
Practical AI Prompts for Avoiding Grant Writing Mistakes 37
- 1. Checking Proposal Alignment with Grant Guidelines 37
- 2. Strengthening Problem Statements 37
- 3. Enhancing Budget Justifications 37
- 4. Simplifying Overly Technical Language 37
- 5. Ensuring Measurable Objectives 37

Looking Ahead 38
- Reflection Questions: 38

Section 6: Integrating AI into the Grant Writing Process 38
The AI-Powered Grant Writing Workflow 39

Benefits and Limitations of Using AI in Grant Writing 40
Case Study: AI-Assisted Grant Writing for a STEM Education Program 40
Practical AI Prompts for Each Stage of Grant Writing 41
- 1. Finding and Analyzing Grant Opportunities 41
- 2. Drafting Key Proposal Sections 41
- 3. Enhancing Readability and Tone 41
- 4. Budget and Financial Justifications 41
- 5. Final Review and Compliance Check 41

Looking Ahead 41
- Reflection Questions: 42

Section 7: Personalizing AI-Generated Content for Grant Proposals 42
Why Personalization Matters in Grant Writing 42
How to Personalize AI-Generated Content 43
- 1. Infuse Organizational Voice and Mission 43
- 2. Include Real-Life Stories and Testimonials 43
- 3. Customize for the Funder's Priorities 43
- 4. Refine Tone and Engagement 43
- 5. Add Passion and Conviction 44

Case Study: How Personalization Transformed an AI-Written Grant Proposal 44
Practical AI Prompts for Enhancing Personal Engagement 45
- 1. Aligning with the Funder's Mission 45
- 2. Infusing Passion and Urgency 45
- 3. Incorporating Human-Centered Storytelling 45
- 4. Refining for Clarity and Engagement 45
- 5. Adding a Strong Call to Action 45

Looking Ahead 45
- Reflection Questions: 45

Section 8: Finalizing and Submitting AI-Enhanced Grant Proposals 46
Key Steps in Finalizing a Grant Proposal 47
How AI Can Assist in the Final Proposal Review 48
Case Study: How AI Helped Perfect a Grant Proposal Before Submission... 48
Practical AI Prompts for Finalizing Grant Proposals 49
- 1. Checking for Clarity and Readability 49
- 2. Summarizing for a Final Review 49

  3. Verifying Alignment with Funder Priorities 49

  4. Proofreading for Grammar and Tone 49

  5. Reviewing Budget Justifications 49

Best Practices for Submitting Grant Proposals 50

Looking Ahead 50

  Reflection Questions: 50

Section 9: Following Up After Grant Submission 51

Why Follow-Up Matters in Grant Writing 51

Grant Follow-Up Scenarios and Best Practices 52

  Scenario 1: The Grant is Awarded 🎉 52

  Scenario 2: The Funder Requests Modifications 📝 52

  Scenario 3: The Grant is Rejected ❌ 52

Case Study: How AI Helped Improve a Resubmitted Grant Proposal 53

Practical AI Prompts for Grant Follow-Up 53

  1. Thanking the Funder After Grant Approval 53

  2. Requesting Feedback After a Grant Rejection 53

  3. Resubmitting an Improved Grant Proposal 53

  4. Finding Alternative Funding Opportunities 54

  5. Providing Progress Updates to Funders 54

Looking Ahead 54

  Reflection Questions: 54

Section 10: Preparing for Future Grant Applications 54

Building a Sustainable Grant Writing Strategy 55

How AI Can Help with Long-Term Grant Planning 56

Case Study: How AI Helped a Nonprofit Build a Long-Term Grant Strategy 56

Practical AI Prompts for Future Grant Planning 57

  1. Tracking Grant Opportunities 57

  2. Analyzing Past Proposal Performance 57

  3. Automating a Grant Calendar 57

  4. Preparing Impact Reports for Funders 57

  5. Refining Proposal Sections for Future Applications 57

Final Thoughts: Mastering Grant Writing with AI 58

Looking Ahead to Chapter 2 58

  Reflection Questions: 58

Chapter 1 Summary: Key Takeaways 58

Chapter 2: AI Tools and Techniques for Grant Writing Success 59

Section 1: Overview of AI in Grant Writing 59

How AI is Changing Grant Writing 59
Types of AI Tools for Grant Writing 60
AI's Strengths and Limitations in Grant Writing 60
Case Study: AI-Powered Grant Proposal Optimization 61
Practical AI Prompts for Enhancing Grant Writing 61
    1. Finding Grant Opportunities 61
    2. Refining Problem Statements 61
    3. Improving Budget Justifications 62
    4. Enhancing Readability and Engagement 62
    5. Checking Grant Proposal Compliance 62

Looking Ahead 62
    Reflection Questions: 62
    Chapter 2, Section 1 Summary 62

Section 2: Best AI Tools for Grant Research and Writing 63

AI Tools for Grant Research and Identification 63
AI Tools for Grant Proposal Writing and Optimization 64
How to Use AI for Grant Research and Writing 64
Case Study: How AI Improved Grant Research and Writing 65
Practical AI Prompts for Grant Research and Writing 66
    1. Finding Grant Opportunities 66
    2. Summarizing Grant Requirements 66
    3. Drafting a Problem Statement 66
    4. Refining Proposal Language 66
    5. Checking Proposal Alignment with Funders 66

Looking Ahead 66
    Reflection Questions: 66
    Chapter 2, Section 2 Summary 67

Section 3: Using AI for Storytelling and Impact in Grant Proposals . 67

Why Storytelling is Crucial in Grant Proposals 67
How AI Can Enhance Storytelling in Grant Proposals 68
Best Practices for Writing Compelling Impact Statements 68

- 1. Start with a Powerful Hook 68
- 2. Use Real Stories and Testimonials 68
- 3. Show Data-Driven Impact 69
- 4. Create a Vision for the Future 69

Case Study: How AI Helped Strengthen Storytelling in a Grant Proposal..... 69

Practical AI Prompts for Enhancing Storytelling and Impact 70

- 1. Crafting a Compelling Hook 70
- 2. Creating a Success Story 70
- 3. Refining an Impact Statement 70
- 4. Strengthening Data Storytelling 70
- 5. Writing a Future-Focused Conclusion 70

Looking Ahead 71

- Reflection Questions: 71
- Chapter 2, Section 3 Summary 71

Section 4: Optimizing Grant Budgets and Financial Justifications with AI 71

Why Budgets and Financial Justifications Matter in Grant Proposals 72

Common Budgeting Mistakes and How to Avoid Them 72

How AI Can Assist in Budget Planning and Justification 73

Best Practices for Writing a Persuasive Budget Justification 73

- 1. Clearly Define Each Budget Category 73
- 2. Use Realistic and Justifiable Costs 73
- 3. Align the Budget with Project Goals 74
- 4. Justify Indirect Costs and Administrative Expenses 74

Case Study: How AI Helped Improve a Grant Budget Justification 74

Practical AI Prompts for Grant Budget Optimization 75

- 1. Structuring a Budget Template 75
- 2. Creating a Justification for Personnel Costs 75
- 3. Breaking Down Equipment or Supply Costs 75
- 4. Explaining Indirect Costs 75
- 5. Checking Budget Alignment with Proposal Objectives 75

Looking Ahead 76

- Reflection Questions: 76
- Chapter 2, Section 4 Summary 76

Section 5: Enhancing Collaboration and Workflow in Grant Writing with AI   76

How AI Enhances Collaboration in Grant Writing 77
AI Tools for Streamlining Grant Writing Collaboration 77
Best Practices for Team-Based AI-Assisted Grant Writing 78
- 1. Define Roles and Responsibilities 78
- 2. Use AI to Ensure Consistency in Writing Style 78
- 3. Automate Project Management with AI 78
- 4. Enable AI-Assisted Feedback and Revisions 79
- 5. Create AI-Generated Meeting Summaries and Action Items 79

Case Study: How AI Improved Team Collaboration in Grant Writing 79
Practical AI Prompts for Optimizing Team Collaboration in Grant Writing 80
- 1. Assigning Roles and Responsibilities 80
- 2. Ensuring Writing Consistency 80
- 3. Automating Task Assignments 80
- 4. AI-Assisted Proposal Review 80
- 5. Generating Meeting Summaries and Next Steps 80

Looking Ahead 81
- Reflection Questions: 81
- Chapter 2, Section 5 Summary 81

Section 6: AI-Assisted Proposal Finalization and Submission Best Practices   81

The Final Steps Before Submitting a Grant Proposal 82
How AI Enhances Proofreading, Compliance, and Document Formatting . 83
Best Practices for a Seamless Submission Process 83
- 1. Submit Early to Avoid Last-Minute Issues 83
- 2. Verify All Required Attachments Are Included 84
- 3. Double-Check Formatting Requirements 84
- 4. Ensure Digital Submission Confirmation 84
- 5. Keep a Copy of the Submitted Proposal for Future Reference 84

Case Study: How AI Helped Perfect a Grant Proposal Before Submission ... 85
Practical AI Prompts for Finalizing and Submitting Grant Proposals 85
- 1. Checking for Clarity and Readability 85
- 2. Verifying Alignment with Funder Priorities 85
- 3. Formatting and Compliance Review 86
- 4. Creating a Submission Checklist 86
- 5. Writing a Submission Confirmation Email 86

Looking Ahead 86
Reflection Questions: 86
Chapter 2, Section 6 Summary 86

Section 7: AI for Post-Submission Follow-Ups, Reporting, and Future Grant
Best Practices for Post-Submission Follow-Ups 87
How AI Can Automate Grant Reporting and Impact Tracking 88
Strategies for Future Grant Planning Using AI 88
Case Study: How AI Helped Optimize Post-Submission Grant Reporting and Planning   89
Practical AI Prompts for Follow-Up, Reporting, and Future Grant Planning 89
1. Writing a Grant Award Thank-You Email 89
2. Requesting Feedback After a Grant Rejection 89
3. Generating a Progress Report for Funders 90
4. Identifying Alternative Funding Sources 90
5. Automating a Grant Submission Calendar 90
Looking Ahead 90
Reflection Questions: 90
Chapter 2, Section 7 Summary 90

Section 8: The Future of AI in Grant Writing – Emerging Trends and Innovations 91
Emerging AI Trends in Grant Writing 91
Innovative AI Applications for Grant Writing and Funding Acquisition 92
Ethical Considerations and Responsible AI Use in Grant Writing 93
Case Study: How AI-Powered Innovations Transformed Grant Writing for a Nonprofit   93
Practical AI Prompts for Staying Ahead in Grant Writing Innovation 94
1. Finding AI-Optimized Grant Opportunities 94
2. Automating Funder Relationship Management 94
3. Predicting Grant Success Likelihood 94
4. Enhancing Proposal Presentation with AI-Generated Visuals 94
5. Ensuring Ethical AI Use in Grant Writing 94
Looking Ahead 95
Reflection Questions: 95
Chapter 2, Section 8 Summary 95

Chapter 3: Implementing AI-Driven Grant Writing Strategies for Different Industries 96

Section 1: How AI Adapts to Industry-Specific Grant Writing Needs 96
How AI Adapts to Different Industry Grant Writing Needs 96

Industry-Specific Funding Sources and Considerations 97
    1. Education (K-12 & Higher Education) 🎓 97
    2. Healthcare & Medical Research ✚ 97
    3. Nonprofits & Community Development 🤝 98
    4. Environmental & Sustainability Grants 🌍 98
    5. Technology & Innovation Startups 🚀 98
    6. Arts, Culture, and Humanities 🎭 99

How AI Customizes Grant Proposals for Each Industry 99

Case Study: AI-Driven Grant Writing Success in Higher Education 100

Practical AI Prompts for Industry-Specific Grant Writing 100
    1. Tailoring Problem Statements 100
    2. Customizing Impact Metrics 100
    3. Ensuring Compliance with Sector Guidelines 101
    4. Adapting Budget Justifications to Industry Standards 101
    5. Finding Industry-Specific Grants 101

Looking Ahead 101
    Reflection Questions: 101
    Chapter 3, Section 1 Summary 101

Section 2: Case Studies and Success Stories of AI-Powered Grant Writing   102

Case Study 1: AI-Optimized Grant Proposal Earns $3 Million for STEM Education Expansion 102

Case Study 2: AI Streamlines Grant Process for Nonprofit Food Security Program 103

Case Study 3: AI-Driven Grant Strategy Boosts Healthcare Research Funding 104

Lessons Learned from AI-Driven Grant Writing Success 105

Practical AI Prompts for Applying Case Study Insights 105
    1. Enhancing Data-Driven Justifications 105
    2. Structuring a High-Impact Problem Statement 105
    3. Automating Budget Formatting & Justification 105
    4. Improving Narrative Storytelling 106
    5. Ensuring Compliance with Funder Guidelines 106

Looking Ahead 106
    Reflection Questions: 106
    Chapter 3, Section 2 Summary 106

Section 3: Building an AI-Powered Grant Writing Workflow from Start to Finish   107

Step-by-Step AI-Powered Grant Writing Workflow
Stage 1: Research & Grant Identification
AI Tools & Strategies:
Stage 2: Planning & Structuring the Proposal
AI Tools & Strategies:
Stage 3: Drafting Proposal Sections
AI Tools & Strategies:
Stage 4: Editing & Refining the Proposal
AI Tools & Strategies:
Stage 5: Budget Development & Justification
AI Tools & Strategies:
Stage 6: Final Review & Submission
AI Tools & Strategies:

Case Study: AI-Powered Workflow Increases Grant Efficiency for a Nonprofit
Practical AI Prompts for Building an AI-Powered Grant Workflow
1. Automating Grant Research
2. Structuring the Proposal Outline
3. Drafting Key Proposal Sections
4. Enhancing Clarity & Compliance
5. Creating a Submission Checklist

What's Next?
Reflection Questions:
Chapter 3, Section 3 Summary

Section 4: Measuring AI's Impact on Grant Writing Success
Key Performance Indicators (KPIs) for Evaluating AI's Effectiveness
How AI-Driven Grant Writing Improves Success Rates
Techniques for Analyzing AI's Impact on Grant Workflow and Quality
1. Comparative Analysis of AI-Enhanced vs. Non-AI Grant Proposals
2. AI-Powered Grant Writing Time Efficiency Study
3. AI-Driven Proposal Quality Assessment
4. Funder Feedback & AI Adjustments

Case Study: Measuring AI's Impact on a Nonprofit's Grant Success
Practical AI Prompts for Assessing Grant Performance and Optimization
1. Evaluating Grant Submission Efficiency

2. Measuring Grant Approval Success Rates 115
  3. Improving Proposal Clarity and Readability 115
  4. Enhancing Budget Transparency for Funders 115
  5. Identifying Patterns in Rejected Grant Applications 115
 Looking Ahead 116
  Reflection Questions: 116
  Chapter 3, Section 4 Summary 116
Section 5: Best Practices for Continuous Improvement in AI-Enhanced Grant Writing 116
 Best Practices for Continuous AI-Enhanced Grant Writing Improvement ... 117
 How to Refine AI-Driven Grant Writing Workflows Over Time 117
  1. Conduct Regular AI Performance Reviews 117
  2. Update AI Tools with New Industry Data 118
  3. Customize AI Outputs Based on Funder Preferences 118
  4. Balance AI Automation with Human-Led Creativity 118
  5. Implement AI-Driven Proposal A/B Testing 118
 AI Tools for Ongoing Learning and Enhancement 119
 Case Study: How Continuous AI Refinement Improved Grant Success 120
 Practical AI Prompts for Optimizing Grant Writing Strategies 120
  1. Improving AI Proposal Quality Based on Past Success 120
  2. Enhancing AI-Generated Impact Statements 120
  3. Customizing Proposals for Different Funders 121
  4. Tracking Grant Performance Metrics 121
  5. Refining Budget Justifications with AI 121
 Looking Ahead 121
  Reflection Questions: 121
  Chapter 3, Section 5 Summary 121
Chapter 4: Overcoming Challenges and Pitfalls in AI-Driven Grant Writing 122
 Section 1: Common Challenges When Using AI for Grant Writing ... 122
 Common Challenges in AI-Driven Grant Writing 123
 The Role of Human Oversight in AI-Generated Grant Writing 123
 How to Recognize and Address AI-Related Pitfalls 124
  1. Avoiding AI-Generated Repetition & Generic Content 124
  2. Ensuring Grant Compliance & Formatting Accuracy 124

    3. Preventing Data Privacy Risks in AI-Powered Grant Writing 124

    4. Improving AI Alignment with Funder Priorities 124

Case Study: Overcoming AI Limitations in Grant Writing 124

Practical AI Prompts for Troubleshooting Grant Writing Issues 125

    1. Identifying and Fixing Repetitive AI-Generated Content 125

    2. Ensuring Compliance with Funder Guidelines 125

    3. Enhancing Emotional Impact in AI-Generated Text 125

    4. Securing Confidential Information in AI-Generated Proposals 125

    5. Improving AI Alignment with Funder Priorities 126

Looking Ahead 126

    Reflection Questions: 126

    Chapter 4, Section 1 Summary 126

Section 2: Navigating Ethical Considerations and Responsible AI Use in Grant Writing 127

Key Ethical Considerations in AI-Powered Grant Writing 127

Best Practices for Responsible AI Use in Grant Writing 128

    1. Disclosing AI Assistance in Proposal Writing 128

    2. Protecting Sensitive Grant Data 128

    3. Addressing Bias in AI-Generated Proposals 128

    4. Ensuring Ethical Storytelling in AI-Assisted Proposals 128

    5. Conducting AI-Assisted Plagiarism and Originality Checks 129

How to Balance AI Efficiency with Human Judgment 129

Case Study: Ethical AI Use in Nonprofit Grant Writing 129

Practical AI Prompts for Ensuring Ethical Grant Writing 130

    1. Reviewing AI-Generated Proposals for Accuracy 130

    2. Ensuring Inclusivity & Bias-Free Language 130

    3. Creating an AI Transparency Disclosure for Funders 130

    4. Strengthening Ethical Impact Statements 131

    5. Implementing AI Security Best Practices in Grant Writing 131

Looking Ahead 131

    Reflection Questions: 131

    Chapter 4, Section 2 Summary 131

Section 3: Troubleshooting AI-Generated Grant Proposals for Clarity, Compliance, and Effectiveness 132

Common Issues in AI-Generated Grant Proposals 132

Techniques for Improving Clarity, Compliance, and Effectiveness 133
- 1. Eliminating Generic & Repetitive Language 133
- 2. Strengthening Emotional Appeal & Storytelling 133
- 3. Ensuring Grant Compliance & Formatting Accuracy 133
- 4. Refining Problem Statements with Data-Driven Justifications 133
- 5. Improving Budget Justifications for Funders 134

How to Fine-Tune AI Prompts for Better Proposal Outputs 135
Example: Weak vs. Strong AI Prompts for Grant Writing 135

Case Study: Troubleshooting AI-Generated Grant Proposals for a Nonprofit 136

Practical AI Prompts for Troubleshooting Grant Writing Issues 136
- 1. Fixing Repetitive or Generic Language in AI-Generated Text 136
- 2. Strengthening Impact Statements with Emotional Appeal 136
- 3. Ensuring Compliance with Funder Guidelines 137
- 4. Refining Budget Justifications for Clarity and Transparency 137
- 5. Improving Problem Statements with Data and Urgency 137

Looking Ahead 137
Reflection Questions: 137
Chapter 4, Section 3 Summary 137

Section 4: Real-World Success Stories and Lessons Learned from AI-Powered Grant Writing 138

Case Study 1: AI Helps Nonprofit Secure $1.2 Million in Housing Grants ... 138

Case Study 2: AI Speeds Up Grant Writing for STEM Education Initiative . 139

Case Study 3: AI Improves Budget Justifications for Healthcare Research Grant 140

Lessons Learned from AI-Powered Grant Writing Success 141

Practical AI Prompts for Applying Lessons to Future Grant Writing 141
- 1. Scaling Grant Writing Without Overburdening Staff 141
- 2. Strengthening Data-Backed Justifications 141
- 3. Creating Funder-Specific Proposal Templates 142
- 4. Improving Budget Justifications for Transparency 142
- 5. Enhancing Proposal Storytelling and Emotional Appeal 142

Looking Ahead 142
Reflection Questions: 142
Chapter 4, Section 4 Summary 143

Chapter 5: Future-Proofing AI-Driven Grant Writing Strategies 144

Section 1: Emerging AI Trends and Innovations in Grant Writing 144
Key Emerging AI Trends in Grant Writing 144
How AI Innovations Are Shaping the Future of Grant Applications 145
  1. AI-Powered Funder Relationship Management........145
  2. Voice-to-Text AI for Grant Drafting 145
  3. AI-Generated Data Visualizations for Grant Proposals.............145
  4. Blockchain-Integrated AI for Grant Transparency 145
  5. AI-Powered Grant Writing Chatbots for Team Collaboration.........145
Potential Risks and Ethical Considerations of Next-Generation AI 146
Practical AI Prompts for Preparing for Future AI Developments in Grant Writing 147
  1. Leveraging Predictive Analytics for Grant Success 147
  2. Automating Grant Writing Workflows with AI..........147
  3. Ensuring Ethical AI Use in Future Grant Writing 147
  4. Preparing for AI-Driven Proposal Personalization 147
  5. AI for Real-Time Proposal Compliance Checks 147
Looking Ahead..........147
  Reflection Questions:........147
  Chapter 5, Section 1 Summary 148

Section 2: Building an Adaptive AI Strategy for Long-Term Grant Writing Success 148
Key Components of a Long-Term AI Strategy for Grant Writing.........149
How to Continuously Refine AI Use for Grant Applications 149
  Step 1: Evaluate AI Performance After Each Grant Submission..........149
  Step 2: Update AI Training Data with New Funding Trends 150
  Step 3: Implement A/B Testing for AI-Generated Grant Proposals 150
  Step 4: Enhance AI Personalization for Different Funders 150
  Step 5: Track AI-Driven Grant Success Metrics Over Time........150
AI-Powered Tools & Frameworks for Sustainable Grant Writing Success 151
Case Study: Implementing an Adaptive AI Grant Writing Strategy for a Nonprofit 151
Practical AI Prompts for Developing an Adaptive AI Strategy 152
  1. Creating an AI-Integrated Grant Writing Workflow........152
  2. Using AI to Improve Long-Term Grant Writing Success..........152
  3. Tracking Grant Writing Performance Metrics 152
  4. Refining AI Personalization for Funder Alignment..........152
  5. Ensuring Ethical & Responsible AI Use in Long-Term Strategy 153

Looking Ahead 153
    Reflection Questions: 153
    Chapter 5, Section 2 Summary 153

Section 3: Training Your Team to Effectively Use AI for Grant Writing 154
Why AI Training is Essential for Grant Writing Teams 154
Key Components of an AI Grant Writing Training Program 155
How to Integrate AI Training into an Organization's Workflow 156
    Step 1: Conduct an AI Knowledge Assessment 156
    Step 2: Provide Hands-On AI Training Workshops 156
    Step 3: Implement AI Mentorship & Peer Learning 156
    Step 4: Establish an AI Resource Hub for Continuous Learning 156
    Step 5: Evaluate AI Training Effectiveness & Gather Feedback 156
Case Study: Implementing AI Training for a Grant Writing Team 157
Practical AI Prompts for Training Your Grant Writing Team 157
    1. Teaching AI-Powered Grant Research & Matching 157
    2. Training on AI-Assisted Proposal Drafting 157
    3. Ensuring Ethical AI Use in Grant Writing 158
    4. Improving AI Adoption Across Teams 158
    5. Evaluating AI Training Effectiveness 158
Looking Ahead 158
    Reflection Questions: 158
    Chapter 5, Section 3 Summary 158

Section 4: Measuring AI's Long-Term Impact on Grant Writing Success 159
Key Performance Indicators (KPIs) for Evaluating AI's Impact on Grant Writing 159
How to Track AI-Driven Improvements in Grant Writing Efficiency 160
    1. Compare Pre-AI vs. Post-AI Grant Writing Metrics 160
    2. Monitor Time Savings in Grant Proposal Development 160
    3. Measure AI's Impact on Proposal Quality & Funder Alignment 160
    4. Identify Trends in AI-Driven Grant Success Rates 160
    5. Collect Qualitative Feedback from Grant Writers & Funders 160
AI Tools & Methods for Analyzing Funding Success Rates 161
Case Study: Measuring AI's Long-Term Impact on Grant Writing for a University 161
Practical AI Prompts for Assessing Long-Term AI Performance 162
    1. Monitoring AI's Role in Grant Submission Efficiency 162

2. Measuring AI-Generated Proposal Success Rates 162

3. Tracking AI-Driven Fund Alignment & Proposal Customization 163

4. Identifying Areas for AI Improvement in Grant Writing 163

5. Assessing AI's Impact on Proposal Readability & Persuasiveness 163

Looking Ahead 163

Reflection Questions: 163

Chapter 5, Section 4 Summary 163

Section 5: Strategies for Staying Ahead in AI-Driven Grant Writing .. 164

How to Continuously Adapt to AI Advancements in Grant Writing 164

Best Practices for Long-Term AI Integration in Grant Writing 165

1. Establish AI Governance & Oversight 165

2. Use AI to Track Long-Term Funding Trends 165

3. Automate Routine Grant Writing Tasks to Focus on Strategy 165

4. Invest in AI-Powered Collaboration Tools 165

5. Create an AI-Optimized Proposal Library 166

How to Future-Proof AI-Enhanced Grant Writing Processes 166

Case Study: How a Nonprofit Future-Proofed Its AI-Driven Grant Writing .. 167

Practical AI Prompts for Staying Ahead in AI-Driven Grant Writing 167

1. Tracking AI-Powered Funding Trends 167

2. Preparing for AI's Future Role in Grant Collaboration 167

3. Using AI to Predict Future Grant Success Rates 168

4. Ensuring Ethical AI-Driven Grant Writing Practices 168

5. Optimizing AI for Personalized Funder Engagement 168

Looking Ahead 168

Reflection Questions: 168

Chapter 5, Section 5 Summary 168

Chapter 6: Conclusion & Final Recommendations 169

6.1 Key Takeaways from AI-Driven Grant Writing 169

1. AI Increases Grant Writing Efficiency 169

2. AI Enhances Proposal Quality & Funder Alignment 169

3. AI Helps Organizations Scale Grant Submissions 169

4. Ethical AI Use is Critical for Long-Term Success 170

5. AI-Driven Data Analytics Improve Future Funding Success 170

6.2 Final Recommendations for Maximizing AI's Potential in Grant Writing   171

6.3 Next Steps for Organizations Implementing AI in Grant Writing. 171
- Step 1: Assess Current AI Readiness 171
- Step 2: Select & Implement the Right AI Tools 172
- Step 3: Train Staff for AI-Enhanced Grant Writing 172
- Step 4: Establish AI Performance Tracking Metrics 172
- Step 5: Continuously Optimize AI Grant Writing Workflows 172

6.4 Final Thoughts: The Future of AI in Grant Writing 172

Final Call to Action: Embracing AI for Grant Writing Success 173

Conclusion: The Future of AI in Grant Writing is Now 174
- Are You Ready to Transform Your Grant Writing with AI? 174

Final Reflection Questions 174
- Chapter 6 Summary: AI-Powered Grant Writing Success 174

Appendix: Essential Resources for Grant Writers 175
- 1. AI-Powered Tools for Grant Writing 175
- 2. Grant Research & Funder Matching Platforms 176
- 3. Proposal Writing & Budgeting Guides 177
- 4. Online Courses & Grant Writing Certifications 178
- 5. AI-Powered Writing & Compliance Tools 179
- 6. Grant Writing Communities & Networks 180
  - Final Thoughts 180

About the Author: Anthony J. Fitzpatrick, Ed.D. 181

Chapter 1: Understanding Grants and Funding Sources

Section 1: The Importance of Grants Across Industries

Grants are a powerful funding mechanism that fuels innovation, supports community development, advances research, and strengthens education. Whether in **K-12 education, nonprofit organizations, small businesses, or medical research**, securing grants can mean the difference between launching a transformative project or watching an idea stall due to a lack of funding. However, the competition for grants is fierce. Organizations and individuals must craft compelling, well-structured proposals that clearly articulate their vision, align with funding priorities, and demonstrate measurable impact.

Why Grants Matter

Grants provide **non-repayable funding**, meaning recipients do not need to return the money—unlike loans or venture capital. This makes them an attractive option for individuals, organizations, and institutions seeking financial support for projects, research, and initiatives that drive progress in their respective fields.

Here's why grants are crucial across different industries:

Industry	Impact of Grants
Education	Supports school technology upgrades, curriculum development, and underserved student programs.
Nonprofits	Expands community outreach, funds social programs, and sustains operational costs.
Small Businesses	Provides startup capital, especially in tech, sustainability, and social enterprise.
Scientific Research	Drives innovation in health, medicine, and STEM fields.
Arts & Culture	Funds artistic projects, museum exhibits, and cultural preservation.

Grants do more than just provide funding—they **validate ideas, increase credibility, and open doors to additional funding sources.** Many organizations leverage successful grant awards as proof of their effectiveness, leading to new funding opportunities.

The Challenges of Grant Writing

While grants offer significant benefits, the application process is often **complex, time-consuming, and highly competitive.** Some common challenges include:

- **Strict Eligibility and Compliance Requirements:** Many grants have specific criteria, and failing to meet even one requirement can lead to rejection.
- **Time-Intensive Research and Writing:** Identifying the right grants and crafting a compelling proposal requires extensive effort.
- **Competitive Landscape:** With limited funding and a large pool of applicants, standing out is critical.
- **Complex Budgeting Requirements:** Many grants require detailed financial planning and justifications.

To overcome these challenges, applicants must master the art of **clear, persuasive writing, strategic storytelling, and data-driven decision-making**—a process that has traditionally required significant time and expertise. However, **Generative AI is revolutionizing grant writing by making it more efficient, data-driven, and accessible.**

How AI is Transforming the Grant Writing Process

The rise of **Generative AI**—advanced machine learning models that generate human-like text—has changed how individuals and organizations approach grant writing. AI tools like **ChatGPT, Bard, Claude, and Perplexity** can assist in:

✓ **Identifying relevant grant opportunities** based on specific needs and goals.
✓ **Generating well-structured drafts** that align with grant requirements.
✓ **Enhancing clarity, grammar, and conciseness** in proposal writing.
✓ **Providing data summaries and research insights** to strengthen applications.
✓ **Streamlining budget narratives** and identifying potential funding gaps.

Case Study: How AI Helped a School District Secure a STEM Grant

◆ **Background:** A mid-sized school district sought funding for a **STEM enrichment program** but lacked the internal resources to write a competitive grant proposal.

♦ How AI Helped:

- **Grant Identification:** AI-assisted tools analyzed grant databases and identified a **$250,000 STEM education grant** aligned with the district's needs.
- **Proposal Drafting:** AI-generated a **structured first draft**, including a problem statement, objectives, and expected outcomes.
- **Data Analysis:** AI summarized relevant student performance data to support the funding request.
- **Refinement & Editing:** Human reviewers fine-tuned the AI draft for authenticity and strategic alignment.

♦ Outcome:
The district **won the grant**, securing funding for robotics kits, coding workshops, and STEM field trips.

♦ Key Takeaway:
AI significantly reduced the time required for grant research and writing, allowing educators to focus on program implementation.

Practical AI Prompt Examples for Grant Writing

If you're new to using AI for grant writing, here are some prompts you can try:

1. Finding Grant Opportunities

✦ *"Find upcoming education grants for K-12 schools focused on STEM programs with deadlines in the next six months."*

2. Generating a Problem Statement

✦ *"Generate a problem statement for a grant proposal on expanding after-school tutoring programs for low-income students."*

3. Drafting Key Proposal Sections

✦ *"Write a compelling introduction for a grant proposal seeking funding for a community food pantry."*

4. Budget Justification Assistance

✦ *"Create a budget justification explaining why $10,000 is needed for new classroom technology."*

5. Refining Language for Clarity

✒ *"Improve the clarity and conciseness of this grant proposal summary: [insert text]."*

By integrating these AI tools into your grant writing process, you can **save time, improve proposal quality, and increase your chances of securing funding.**

Looking Ahead

In the next section, we will explore **the different types of grants available**, helping you identify **the right funding sources for your specific needs.**

Reflection Questions:

Consider these questions to apply the concepts in this section to your own grant-writing experience:

1. What funding opportunities are most relevant to your industry or organization?
2. Have you encountered challenges in past grant applications, and how could AI help streamline those areas?
3. How comfortable are you with integrating AI tools into your writing process?

Section 2: Types of Grants and Their Funding Sources

Securing the right grant begins with understanding the different types of funding available. Grants come in various forms, each with its own eligibility requirements, application processes, and funding structures. Whether you're in education, research, business, or nonprofit work, knowing where and how to look for funding increases your chances of success.

This section will break down the **five primary types of grants**, explain their sources, and provide **AI-powered strategies** for identifying the best-fit grants for your needs.

Types of Grants

Grant funding can be broadly categorized into five major types:

Type of Grant	Definition	Example Funding Sources
Government Grants	Publicly funded grants provided by federal, state, or local agencies. Often the most competitive but offer the highest funding amounts.	U.S. Department of Education, National Science Foundation (NSF), Small Business Administration (SBA)
Foundation Grants	Awarded by private or corporate foundations to fund specific social, educational, or research initiatives.	Gates Foundation, Ford Foundation, Kellogg Foundation
Corporate Grants	Provided by businesses as part of their corporate social responsibility (CSR) initiatives. Often focused on education, sustainability, or innovation.	Google Impact Challenge, Microsoft AI for Good, Amazon Future Engineer
Research Grants	Typically awarded to universities, researchers, and institutions to fund scientific, medical, or social science research.	National Institutes of Health (NIH), National Endowment for the Humanities (NEH)
Community Grants	Small-scale grants designed to support grassroots initiatives, local nonprofits, and community programs.	Local government agencies, regional community foundations, United Way

Each grant type requires a **tailored proposal approach** that aligns with the funder's goals and priorities. Understanding these differences is key to writing a competitive application.

How to Identify the Right Type of Grant for Your Project

Before applying for a grant, ask yourself the following:

✓ **What is the primary focus of your project?** (Education, healthcare, business, community impact, research, etc.)
✓ **Who will benefit from the grant funding?** (Students, small businesses, underserved communities, etc.)
✓ **What is the funding range you need?** (Some grants fund small pilot projects, while others support large-scale initiatives.)
✓ **What reporting and compliance requirements can you handle?** (Some funders require extensive follow-up and impact reports.)

Answering these questions will **narrow down** your search for the best-fit grants. AI can further streamline this process by **automating grant discovery** and **matching opportunities to your needs.**

Case Study: How AI Helped a Nonprofit Find the Perfect Grant

♦ **Background:** A nonprofit organization focused on youth mental health wanted to expand its free counseling services in schools but **struggled to identify appropriate funding sources.**

♦ **How AI Helped:**

- **AI-Driven Research:** The organization used ChatGPT to generate a list of **federal and foundation grants** focused on youth mental health.
- **Matching Priorities:** AI scanned grant databases to find funding aligned with the nonprofit's **mission and geographic region.**
- **Proposal Structuring:** AI suggested how to **tailor the application** to match funder priorities.

♦ **Outcome:** The nonprofit applied for a **$100,000 foundation grant** and secured funding to launch its school-based mental health program.

♦ **Key Takeaway:** Using AI reduced the time spent on research from weeks to hours, allowing the organization to focus on writing a compelling application.

Practical AI Prompts for Identifying Grants

1. Finding Government Grants

★ *"Find upcoming federal grants related to STEM education for K-12 schools with a minimum award of $50,000."*

2. Searching for Foundation Grants

★ *"List 10 private foundations that fund early childhood literacy programs."*

3. Identifying Corporate Grants

★ *"Which major companies offer grants for sustainability and environmental projects?"*

4. Matching Grants to Organizational Needs

📌 *"Based on this project description [insert details], recommend grants that align with its goals."*

5. Generating a Summary of Grant Requirements

📌 *"Summarize the eligibility criteria and deadlines for the latest NSF research grants."*

By using AI-driven grant discovery tools, applicants can **save time, identify more funding opportunities, and improve their overall grant strategy.**

Looking Ahead

Now that we've explored **the different types of grants and how to identify them**, the next section will dive into **the essential components of a strong grant proposal**—a crucial step in securing funding.

Reflection Questions:

Consider these questions to personalize your grant search strategy:

1. Which type of grant (government, foundation, corporate, research, or community) best fits your needs?
2. Have you struggled in the past to find grants that align with your project? How might AI streamline this process?
3. What are the next steps in identifying potential funders for your work?

Section 3: The Structure of a Strong Grant Proposal

Securing a grant requires more than just a good idea—it requires **a well-structured proposal that aligns with the funder's goals, follows specific guidelines, and clearly communicates impact.** Grant proposals typically follow a standard format, but the structure may vary depending on the type of grant and funding organization.

This section will break down the **key components of a successful grant proposal**, explain why each section matters, and provide **AI-powered strategies** for improving proposal clarity and effectiveness.

Key Components of a Grant Proposal

While specific grants may have unique requirements, most proposals include the following **core sections**:

Section	Purpose	Key AI-Enhanced Strategies
Cover Letter (if required)	Introduces the proposal and makes a compelling first impression.	Use AI to generate **concise and persuasive introductions** tailored to the funder's mission.
Executive Summary	Provides a high-level overview of the proposal's purpose, goals, and funding request.	AI can draft summaries based on full proposals, ensuring clarity and alignment with grant guidelines.
Problem Statement (Needs Assessment)	Describes the issue the project addresses and why it matters.	AI can assist in **data gathering, trend analysis, and crafting an evidence-based argument.**
Project Goals and Objectives	Clearly defines what the project will achieve and how.	AI can help **convert broad goals into measurable, outcome-focused objectives.**
Methodology (Project Design & Implementation Plan)	Explains how the project will be executed, including timelines and key activities.	AI can generate **structured project plans, workflows, and milestone timelines.**
Evaluation Plan	Details how success will be measured and reported.	AI can help create **evaluation metrics and reporting frameworks.**
Budget and Budget Justification	Provides a financial breakdown of the requested funds and how they will be used.	AI can assist in **drafting budget narratives, identifying gaps, and improving financial clarity.**
Sustainability Plan (if required)	Explains how the project will continue after the grant period ends.	AI can suggest **long-term funding strategies and sustainability models.**
Conclusion	Reinforces the proposal's impact and makes a final appeal for funding.	AI can refine conclusions to **enhance persuasiveness and clarity.**

By ensuring that each section is **clear, data-driven, and aligned with funder priorities**, applicants **increase their chances of winning grants**.

Common Pitfalls and How to Avoid Them

Many grant applications are rejected due to **avoidable mistakes**. Below are common pitfalls and how AI can help address them:

Common Mistake	AI-Enhanced Solution
Vague problem statements	AI can refine **data-driven arguments** using statistics and evidence.
Unclear project objectives	AI can generate **SMART goals** (Specific, Measurable, Achievable, Relevant, Time-bound).
Overly technical language	AI can **simplify complex jargon** to make proposals more accessible.
Weak budget justifications	AI can **break down costs** into clear, funder-friendly narratives.
Failure to align with funder priorities	AI can analyze grant guidelines and **suggest ways to tailor proposals accordingly.**

Case Study: How AI Helped a Small Business Write a Winning Proposal

- **Background:** A small business specializing in **eco-friendly packaging** sought funding from a sustainability-focused grant but struggled to develop a strong, competitive proposal.

- **How AI Helped:**

    - **Drafting a Data-Driven Problem Statement:** AI helped compile research on **plastic waste reduction** and industry trends.
    - **Refining Objectives:** AI structured the proposal's objectives into **clear, measurable outcomes** that aligned with grant priorities.
    - **Strengthening Budget Justification:** AI analyzed project costs and generated a **concise, persuasive budget narrative.**
    - **Editing for Clarity and Impact:** AI enhanced readability, ensuring the proposal was **persuasive yet professional.**

- **Outcome:** The business won a **$75,000 grant** to launch its biodegradable packaging line.

📌 **Key Takeaway:** AI transformed a generic proposal into a targeted, compelling application, increasing the business's chances of securing funding.

Practical AI Prompts for Crafting a Strong Grant Proposal

1. Drafting a Persuasive Problem Statement

📌 *"Write a problem statement for a grant proposal on expanding mental health services for underserved communities. Include relevant statistics and research."*

2. Structuring Project Goals and Objectives

📌 *"Convert the following project description into SMART objectives: [Insert project details]."*

3. Generating a Timeline for Implementation

📌 *"Create a 12-month implementation timeline for a community literacy program, breaking it down by key milestones."*

4. Enhancing Budget Justifications

📌 *"Generate a clear and concise budget justification for a $50,000 grant request covering staff salaries, program materials, and outreach efforts."*

5. Editing and Refining for Clarity

📌 *"Revise this grant proposal section to improve clarity and persuasiveness: [Insert text]."*

Using these AI prompts, applicants can **strengthen their proposals, improve clarity, and better align with funder expectations**.

Looking Ahead

Now that we've covered **how to structure a strong grant proposal**, the next section will explore **the role of data and research in grants**—a crucial element for building credibility and making proposals more compelling.

Reflection Questions:

1. Which sections of a grant proposal have been most challenging for you in the past?
2. How can AI help streamline the writing and structuring of your grant proposal?
3. What specific grant requirements should you focus on improving for your next application?

Section 4: The Role of Data and Research in Grants

A strong grant proposal is not just about compelling storytelling—it must be **rooted in data and evidence**. Funders want to ensure that their investment will yield measurable outcomes, making data a critical component in proving the **need, feasibility, and impact** of a project.

This section will explore:
- ✅ **Why data matters in grant proposals**
- ✅ **Types of research and data to include**
- ✅ **How AI can assist in gathering and analyzing data**
- ✅ **Common mistakes and how to avoid them**

Why Data is Essential in Grant Writing

Funders need **concrete proof** that a problem exists and that the proposed solution will be effective. A well-researched, data-driven proposal:

- 📌 **Establishes credibility** – Demonstrates expertise and a deep understanding of the issue.
- 📌 **Strengthens the problem statement** – Supports claims with statistics and research.
- 📌 **Justifies funding needs** – Shows evidence-based reasoning for the budget request.
- 📌 **Demonstrates potential impact** – Predicts measurable, data-backed outcomes.

Without supporting data, proposals **lack legitimacy and persuasive power**, making them less likely to receive funding.

Types of Data to Include in Grant Proposals

Data Type	Purpose	Example
Needs Assessment Data	Demonstrates the urgency of the problem.	"1 in 5 students in our district lack access to STEM learning resources."
Demographic and Population Data	Provides insights into target beneficiaries.	"80% of program participants come from low-income households."
Previous Program Data	Shows past success and impact.	"Our pilot program increased literacy rates by 30% over two years."
Benchmarking Data	Compares to industry or national standards.	"Nationally, 60% of startups fail within three years; our program reduced this to 40%."
Projected Impact Data	Predicts measurable outcomes of the proposed project.	"We anticipate a 25% increase in student engagement in STEM courses."

Funders **want to see numbers**—not just narratives. Well-integrated data makes proposals **more compelling and evidence-driven**.

How AI Enhances Data Collection and Analysis

AI can **significantly reduce the time** spent on research by automating data collection, summarization, and analysis. Here's how:

AI Capability	How It Helps in Grant Writing
Identifying Key Statistics	AI can extract relevant data from research papers, reports, and open databases.
Summarizing Studies & Reports	AI can generate concise literature reviews from complex academic papers.
Analyzing Trends & Patterns	AI can interpret datasets and highlight key insights.
Creating Data Visualizations	AI tools can transform raw data into charts, graphs, and infographics.

By integrating AI-driven research, grant writers can **enhance proposal credibility, reduce research time, and ensure stronger, data-backed justifications**.

Case Study: AI-Powered Data Analysis for an Educational Grant Proposal

♦ **Background:** A nonprofit wanted to apply for a **$500,000 grant** to expand a literacy program but needed strong data to justify the need and projected impact.

♦ **How AI Helped:**

- **Gathering Needs Assessment Data:** AI scanned **state education reports** to find literacy rates in underserved communities.
- **Benchmarking Against National Averages:** AI compared local reading scores to national standards.
- **Summarizing Research Findings:** AI extracted insights from **peer-reviewed studies** on effective literacy interventions.
- **Creating Data Visualizations:** AI-generated **charts** showcasing literacy gaps and projected improvements.

♦ **Outcome:** The nonprofit **secured the grant** by presenting a compelling, data-driven case that demonstrated both need and impact.

✦ **Key Takeaway:** AI drastically reduced the time spent on research and strengthened the proposal's credibility.

Practical AI Prompts for Data-Driven Grant Writing

1. Finding Relevant Statistics

✒ *"Find the latest statistics on food insecurity among children in urban areas."*

2. Summarizing Research Studies

✒ *"Summarize the key findings of this research paper on STEM education impact: [insert text or link]."*

3. Analyzing Trends and Patterns

✒ *"What are the biggest trends in workforce development funding over the last five years?"*

4. Generating Data Visualizations

✒ *"Create a bar chart comparing high school graduation rates among different socioeconomic groups."*

5. Crafting a Data-Backed Problem Statement

✒ *"Use these statistics to create a compelling problem statement for a grant proposal: [insert data]."*

By using AI for data gathering and analysis, grant writers can **increase the persuasiveness and credibility of their proposals while saving time**.

Looking Ahead

Now that we've covered the **importance of data and research**, the next section will focus on **common grant writing mistakes and how to avoid them**—an essential guide to increasing the chances of funding success.

Reflection Questions:

1. What types of data would strengthen your current or upcoming grant proposals?
2. How could AI help streamline your research process?
3. How can you improve your use of statistics and research to make your proposals more persuasive?

Section 5: Common Grant Writing Mistakes and How to Avoid Them

Grant writing is highly competitive, and even minor mistakes can result in a proposal being rejected. Understanding common pitfalls—and how to avoid them—can significantly improve the chances of securing funding.

This section will explore:
✅ **The most frequent mistakes in grant writing**
✅ **How to fix and avoid these mistakes**
✅ **How AI can help improve proposal clarity and alignment**

Top 5 Common Grant Writing Mistakes and Solutions

Mistake	Why It's a Problem	AI-Enhanced Solution
1. Not Following Grant Guidelines	Funders provide strict instructions, and missing a requirement can lead to automatic disqualification.	AI can analyze grant guidelines and generate a **compliance checklist** to ensure all requirements are met.
2. Weak or Vague Problem Statements	Funders need a clear, data-driven understanding of why funding is necessary.	AI can refine problem statements by incorporating **relevant data, statistics, and research**.
3. Lack of Alignment with Funder Priorities	If the proposal does not clearly align with the funder's mission, it is unlikely to be selected.	AI can cross-reference the proposal with the funder's **stated goals and priorities** to ensure alignment.
4. Poor Budget Justification	If the budget lacks detail, funders may question financial accountability.	AI can **generate clear budget justifications**, ensuring each expense is well-explained.
5. Overly Complex or Unclear Writing	Jargon-filled, wordy, or vague proposals are harder to read and less persuasive.	AI can **simplify language, improve readability, and enhance clarity** while maintaining a professional tone.

Many grant rejections happen **not because the project is weak, but because the proposal lacks clarity, alignment, or precision.** AI tools can help **identify, refine, and correct** these mistakes before submission.

Case Study: How AI Helped Fix a Failing Grant Proposal

◆ **Background:** A small nonprofit applied for a **$150,000 community development grant** but received **negative feedback from reviewers** due to **unclear objectives and a weak problem statement.**

◆ **How AI Helped:**

- **Identifying Weaknesses:** AI analyzed the **reviewer feedback** and highlighted areas needing improvement.
- **Rewriting the Problem Statement:** AI helped **integrate data** to make the case for funding stronger.
- **Clarifying Objectives:** AI refined the **project goals** to be more measurable and aligned with funder priorities.
- **Improving Budget Justification:** AI provided **clearer explanations** for financial allocations.

- **Outcome:** The nonprofit **re-submitted the improved proposal** and secured full funding for its project.

- **Key Takeaway:** AI can serve as a grant-writing coach, identifying problem areas and enhancing clarity and alignment before submission.

Practical AI Prompts for Avoiding Grant Writing Mistakes

1. Checking Proposal Alignment with Grant Guidelines

📌 *"Analyze this grant proposal and compare it to the funder's priorities. Where are the gaps?"*

2. Strengthening Problem Statements

📌 *"Rewrite this problem statement to include relevant data and a more compelling need for funding: [insert text]."*

3. Enhancing Budget Justifications

📌 *"Generate a clear, persuasive budget justification for a $75,000 grant covering staffing, materials, and outreach."*

4. Simplifying Overly Technical Language

📌 *"Rewrite this section to make it clearer and more accessible while maintaining a professional tone: [insert text]."*

5. Ensuring Measurable Objectives

📌 *"Convert these general project goals into SMART (Specific, Measurable, Achievable, Relevant, Time-bound) objectives: [insert goals]."*

By using AI to **identify common mistakes and refine proposals**, applicants can **increase their chances of grant approval**.

Looking Ahead

Now that we've covered **common mistakes and how to avoid them**, the next section will focus on **how AI can be integrated into the grant writing process step-by-step**—helping streamline research, drafting, and editing.

Reflection Questions:

1. Have you ever received feedback on a rejected grant proposal? What mistakes did reviewers highlight?
2. Which of the common mistakes listed in this section do you think AI could help you improve?
3. How can you implement AI-driven review strategies before your next grant submission?

Section 6: Integrating AI into the Grant Writing Process

Grant writing has traditionally been a time-consuming process requiring extensive research, meticulous planning, and persuasive writing. With the advent of **Generative AI**, organizations and individuals can **streamline, enhance, and optimize** every stage of the grant-writing process.

This section will explore:
✅ **How AI fits into each stage of grant writing**
✅ **The benefits and limitations of AI in grant writing**
✅ **How AI can assist with grant research, drafting, and editing**
✅ **Practical AI prompts to use at each stage of the grant process**

The AI-Powered Grant Writing Workflow

AI can assist **at every stage** of the grant writing process, from **identifying funding opportunities** to **finalizing a polished, competitive proposal**. Below is a step-by-step breakdown of how AI can be used effectively.

Stage	*Traditional Approach*	*AI-Enhanced Approach*
1. Identifying Grants	Time-intensive research, manually searching for opportunities.	AI scans **databases and websites** to find grants that match project goals.
2. Analyzing Grant Requirements	Reading lengthy RFPs and extracting key criteria.	AI summarizes **eligibility requirements, deadlines, and key priorities**.
3. Drafting Key Sections	Writing from scratch, requiring significant time and effort.	AI generates **problem statements, objectives, and narratives** based on prompts.
4. Refining Language & Tone	Manual revisions, ensuring clarity and professionalism.	AI improves **grammar, readability, and persuasiveness**.
5. Strengthening Budget Justifications	Ensuring expenses align with grant guidelines.	AI assists in **structuring clear, funder-friendly budget narratives**.
6. Reviewing & Submitting	Peer review and manual checks for completeness.	AI checks for **alignment with funder priorities and identifies potential gaps**.

By **integrating AI strategically**, grant writers can **increase efficiency, enhance proposal quality, and maximize success rates**.

Benefits and Limitations of Using AI in Grant Writing

While AI offers significant advantages, it is important to recognize its limitations and use it as a **supporting tool rather than a replacement for human expertise**.

AI Benefits	AI Limitations
Saves time by automating repetitive tasks.	May generate **generic or overly broad** content if not guided properly.
Enhances clarity and readability.	Can lack **emotional depth and personal connection** in writing.
Helps identify relevant funding opportunities.	Requires **human verification** of data accuracy.
Improves budget justifications and impact statements.	May misinterpret **complex grant requirements** if not reviewed carefully.

The key to using AI effectively in grant writing is **balancing automation with human insight and expertise**.

Case Study: AI-Assisted Grant Writing for a STEM Education Program

- **Background:** A school district was applying for a **$250,000 federal grant** to expand its STEM education curriculum but had limited internal capacity to write a strong proposal.

- **How AI Helped:**

  - **Grant Research:** AI identified **three additional funding sources** that the district had not previously considered.
  - **Drafting Key Sections:** AI generated **a structured problem statement and project goals** based on input from school administrators.
  - **Refining the Narrative:** AI **enhanced clarity and persuasiveness**, ensuring alignment with grant guidelines.
  - **Budget Justification:** AI provided **a well-structured breakdown of expenses**, making the proposal more funder-friendly.

- **Outcome:** The district **secured full funding** and now plans to expand its STEM labs and coding workshops.

✦ **Key Takeaway:** AI significantly reduced the time required to draft a high-quality, competitive proposal, allowing staff to focus on program development.

Practical AI Prompts for Each Stage of Grant Writing

1. Finding and Analyzing Grant Opportunities

📌 *"Find upcoming federal grants related to community healthcare programs with deadlines in the next six months."*
📌 *"Summarize the key eligibility requirements for this grant: [insert grant details]."*

2. Drafting Key Proposal Sections

📌 *"Write a compelling problem statement for a grant proposal focused on expanding mental health services in high schools."*
📌 *"Generate three SMART objectives for a workforce development grant proposal."*

3. Enhancing Readability and Tone

📌 *"Rewrite this section to improve clarity and conciseness while maintaining a professional tone: [insert text]."*

4. Budget and Financial Justifications

📌 *"Generate a detailed budget justification for a $50,000 grant covering staff training, program materials, and marketing."*

5. Final Review and Compliance Check

📌 *"Analyze this proposal and identify areas where it does not align with the grant's stated priorities."*
📌 *"Check for jargon and simplify complex language in this grant proposal: [insert text]."*

By using AI **at each stage** of the grant writing process, applicants can **increase efficiency, strengthen proposal quality, and improve alignment with funder expectations**.

Looking Ahead

Now that we've covered **how to integrate AI into the grant writing process**, the next section will focus on **how to personalize AI-generated content**—ensuring that proposals remain compelling, human-centered, and engaging for funders.

Reflection Questions:

1. What stage of the grant writing process is most time-consuming for you?
2. How can AI streamline and optimize your workflow?
3. What specific AI tools or strategies would you like to explore further?

Section 7: Personalizing AI-Generated Content for Grant Proposals

While **AI is a powerful tool** for streamlining grant writing, its outputs can sometimes lack the **human touch** that funders look for. A grant proposal should be **clear, compelling, and aligned with the funder's mission**, which requires **personalization beyond AI-generated text**.

This section will explore:
- **Why personalization is essential in grant writing**
- **Strategies for humanizing AI-generated content**
- **Balancing AI efficiency with authenticity**
- **Practical AI prompts for enhancing personal engagement**

Why Personalization Matters in Grant Writing

Funders are not just looking for well-written proposals—they want to see a **genuine connection** between the applicant and the funding organization. A generic, AI-generated proposal can fall flat if it lacks:

- **Emotional resonance** – Funders want to feel the passion behind the project.
- **Mission alignment** – The proposal should reflect shared values and priorities.
- **A clear, compelling voice** – Proposals should sound human, not robotic.
- **Specific examples and storytelling** – Real-world impact stories are more persuasive than general statements.

AI can assist in **drafting strong content**, but human input is necessary to **personalize and refine the final proposal**.

How to Personalize AI-Generated Content

Here are key strategies for adding **a human touch** to AI-assisted grant writing:

1. Infuse Organizational Voice and Mission

💡 **AI Tip:** Provide AI with information about your organization's values, goals, and tone before generating content.

✅ **Example AI Prompt:**
📌 *"Rewrite this project description to better reflect the mission of [organization name], which focuses on [insert core mission, e.g., equity in education]."*

2. Include Real-Life Stories and Testimonials

💡 **AI Tip:** Use AI to structure impact stories, but add **authentic quotes and details** to enhance credibility.

✅ **Example AI Prompt:**
📌 *"Generate a success story about how an after-school program helped a student improve literacy skills, using this data: [insert key details]."*

3. Customize for the Funder's Priorities

💡 **AI Tip:** AI can analyze funder priorities, but human review ensures deeper alignment.

✅ **Example AI Prompt:**
📌 *"Rewrite this proposal introduction to better reflect the priorities of [funder's name], which emphasizes [insert focus area, e.g., workforce development]."*

4. Refine Tone and Engagement

💡 **AI Tip:** AI-generated text can be **formal and generic**—adjusting tone makes proposals more engaging.

✅ **Example AI Prompt:**
📌 *"Make this executive summary more engaging and persuasive while keeping it professional."*

5. Add Passion and Conviction

💡 **AI Tip:** AI can structure arguments, but human touch **adds urgency and excitement** to proposals.

✓ **Example AI Prompt:**
📌 *"Revise this problem statement to sound more passionate and urgent, emphasizing the real-world impact."*

By **customizing AI-generated content**, grant writers can **maximize efficiency while maintaining a personal, compelling narrative**.

Case Study: How Personalization Transformed an AI-Written Grant Proposal

♦ **Background:** A nonprofit organization applied for a **$200,000 social impact grant** to support **mental health services for underserved youth**.

♦ **Problem:** The first AI-generated draft was **well-structured but lacked emotional depth** and a strong connection to the funder's mission.

♦ **How Personalization Improved the Proposal:**

- **Adding Real Stories:** The team **incorporated a student success story** to illustrate the program's impact.
- **Aligning with Funder's Values:** The proposal was **rewritten to emphasize mental health equity**, a key funder priority.
- **Refining Tone:** AI-assisted edits made the proposal **more engaging and less robotic**.

♦ **Outcome:** The personalized proposal **won the grant**, securing full funding for program expansion.

♦ **Key Takeaway:** AI can draft strong proposals, but personalization and human refinement make them truly compelling.

Practical AI Prompts for Enhancing Personal Engagement

1. Aligning with the Funder's Mission

📌 *"Rewrite this proposal to highlight how it aligns with [funder's name]'s mission of [insert focus area]."*

2. Infusing Passion and Urgency

📌 *"Make this problem statement more compelling and urgent, emphasizing the real-world impact."*

3. Incorporating Human-Centered Storytelling

📌 *"Create a narrative about a community member who benefited from our program, using this data: [insert details]."*

4. Refining for Clarity and Engagement

📌 *"Revise this section to sound more natural and engaging while maintaining professionalism."*

5. Adding a Strong Call to Action

📌 *"Write a persuasive closing statement that reinforces why this project deserves funding."*

By **balancing AI-generated efficiency with human personalization**, grant writers can create **highly compelling, funder-aligned proposals**.

Looking Ahead

Now that we've covered **how to personalize AI-generated content**, the next section will focus on **finalizing and submitting AI-enhanced grant proposals**—ensuring that proposals meet all requirements and maximize funding success.

Reflection Questions:

1. How can you add more personalization to your AI-assisted grant proposals?
2. Which strategies in this section could help you make your proposals more engaging?
3. What are the next steps in refining your AI-enhanced writing process?

Section 8: Finalizing and Submitting AI-Enhanced Grant Proposals

Once a grant proposal is drafted and personalized, the final step is to **ensure its accuracy, completeness, and alignment with funder expectations** before submission. This stage is crucial because even the most compelling proposal can be rejected due to minor errors, missing information, or formatting issues.

This section will explore:
- ✓ **How to conduct a final review of an AI-enhanced proposal**
- ✓ **AI-powered tools for proofreading and compliance checks**
- ✓ **Submission best practices for maximizing funding success**
- ✓ **Practical AI prompts for finalizing grant proposals**

Key Steps in Finalizing a Grant Proposal

Before submitting a proposal, ensure that it is **thoroughly reviewed, aligned with grant guidelines, and free of errors**. Below is a step-by-step checklist:

Final Review Step	*Why It's Important*	*AI-Powered Assistance*
1. Check Grant Guidelines Compliance	Proposals must strictly follow funder requirements (word count, format, attachments).	AI can generate a **compliance checklist** to verify adherence to requirements.
2. Proofread for Clarity and Grammar	Typos, awkward phrasing, or unclear sentences can weaken a proposal.	AI can conduct **grammar and readability checks** to enhance clarity.
3. Verify Data Accuracy	Inaccurate statistics or misrepresented figures can undermine credibility.	AI can cross-check data against **public databases and research reports**.
4. Ensure Alignment with Funder's Priorities	Proposals should directly reflect the mission and goals of the funder.	AI can analyze the proposal against the funder's **mission statement** to suggest refinements.
5. Strengthen Budget Justifications	Budgets must be clear, reasonable, and fully justified.	AI can refine **budget narratives** and identify **missing details**.
6. Improve Readability and Engagement	The proposal should be persuasive and easy to follow.	AI can **restructure complex sentences** and improve **flow and engagement**.
7. Conduct a Final Human Review	AI cannot replace human intuition and industry knowledge.	Use AI to **generate a summary**, then review manually for **tone and accuracy**.

Following these **review steps** ensures that proposals are **polished, persuasive, and ready for submission**.

How AI Can Assist in the Final Proposal Review

AI tools can **speed up and improve** the final review process by assisting in **proofreading, compliance checks, and quality enhancement**.

AI Function	How It Helps in Finalizing Proposals
Grammar and Clarity Check	AI tools like Grammarly, ChatGPT, and Bard help improve clarity and readability.
Compliance Verification	AI can cross-check the proposal against funder guidelines to ensure all requirements are met.
Data Fact-Checking	AI can compare proposal statistics with publicly available data sources for accuracy.
Summarization for Final Review	AI can generate a concise summary, allowing human reviewers to assess alignment with grant priorities.

By combining AI-powered tools with **human expertise**, applicants can submit **high-quality, error-free proposals** that maximize their chances of funding success.

Case Study: How AI Helped Perfect a Grant Proposal Before Submission

- **Background:** A research team applying for a **$500,000 NIH grant** needed to finalize and polish their proposal **within 48 hours** before the deadline.

- **Challenges:**

  - The draft was **too long** and exceeded the word limit.
  - The **budget justification was incomplete**.
  - Some sections lacked **clarity and engagement**.

- **How AI Helped:**

  - **Summarization & Editing:** AI condensed sections **without losing critical details** to fit within the word count.
  - **Budget Refinement:** AI **filled in missing budget justifications**, ensuring transparency and funder alignment.

- **Readability Enhancement:** AI improved clarity, **eliminating redundant phrases and enhancing persuasiveness**.

♦ **Outcome:** The team submitted the revised proposal **on time** and successfully **advanced to the next funding stage**.

♦ **Key Takeaway:** AI-enhanced final reviews can help refine, streamline, and ensure compliance in last-minute grant submissions.

Practical AI Prompts for Finalizing Grant Proposals

1. Checking for Clarity and Readability

📌 *"Analyze this proposal and suggest edits to improve clarity and readability."*

2. Summarizing for a Final Review

📌 *"Generate a 300-word summary of this grant proposal highlighting key objectives and impact."*

3. Verifying Alignment with Funder Priorities

📌 *"Compare this proposal with the stated priorities of [funder's name] and suggest ways to improve alignment."*

4. Proofreading for Grammar and Tone

📌 *"Check this text for grammatical errors, awkward phrasing, and readability improvements."*

5. Reviewing Budget Justifications

📌 *"Evaluate this budget justification and suggest ways to make it clearer and more compelling."*

Using AI for the **final review process** ensures that grant proposals are **polished, professional, and submission-ready**.

Best Practices for Submitting Grant Proposals

Beyond finalizing the content, **submission logistics** play a key role in grant success. Here are some best practices:

- ✅ **Submit Early** – Avoid last-minute technical issues by submitting at least **48 hours before the deadline**.
- ✅ **Double-Check Attachments** – Ensure all required documents (budgets, letters of support, appendices) are included.
- ✅ **Follow Submission Instructions** – Adhere to **specific formatting, font, and file type requirements** set by the funder.
- ✅ **Save and Back Up Your Work** – Maintain multiple copies of your proposal in case of submission errors.
- ✅ **Confirm Receipt** – If applicable, request a confirmation email to ensure successful submission.

By following these **submission best practices**, applicants can avoid technical errors and **increase their chances of funding success**.

Looking Ahead

Now that we've covered **finalizing and submitting AI-enhanced grant proposals**, the next section will explore **strategies for following up after submission**—including best practices for handling rejections and resubmissions.

Reflection Questions:

1. How can AI help you refine your grant proposals before submission?
2. What are the most challenging aspects of finalizing a proposal, and how can AI streamline these tasks?
3. How can you improve your grant submission process to increase efficiency and accuracy?

Section 9: Following Up After Grant Submission

Submitting a grant proposal is only the beginning of the funding journey. A strong **follow-up strategy** can demonstrate professionalism, reinforce relationships with funders, and improve future proposals—whether the grant is approved or rejected.

This section will explore:
- ✅ **Best practices for following up after submission**
- ✅ **How to handle grant acceptance, modification requests, and rejections**
- ✅ **Using AI for follow-up emails, impact reports, and resubmission strategies**
- ✅ **Practical AI prompts for effective grant follow-up**

Why Follow-Up Matters in Grant Writing

Grant writing is more than just a one-time submission—it's about **building long-term relationships** with funders. A well-planned follow-up strategy can:

📌 **Increase chances of future funding** – Even if a proposal is rejected, funders may consider revised applications.
📌 **Provide clarity on proposal strengths and weaknesses** – Feedback helps improve future grant writing efforts.
📌 **Show commitment to project success** – Funders appreciate organizations that communicate progress and impact.
📌 **Establish relationships for future opportunities** – Strong connections with funders can lead to additional funding streams.

Following up **professionally and strategically** can **open doors for future funding**—even if the initial grant is not awarded.

Grant Follow-Up Scenarios and Best Practices

There are three key scenarios that follow a grant submission:

Scenario 1: The Grant is Awarded 🎉

✅ **Next Steps:**

- **Express Gratitude:** Send a formal thank-you letter to the funder.
- **Review Award Terms:** Ensure you understand reporting requirements and compliance expectations.
- **Develop an Implementation Plan:** Start executing the project and keep funders updated.

✅ **How AI Can Help:**
📌 *"Draft a professional thank-you email to a funder after receiving a grant award."*

Scenario 2: The Funder Requests Modifications ✍️

✅ **Next Steps:**

- **Clarify the Requested Changes:** Contact the funder for additional details if needed.
- **Revise and Resubmit Quickly:** Address requested changes while ensuring proposal clarity.
- **Reaffirm Alignment with Funder Goals:** Show commitment to meeting funder expectations.

✅ **How AI Can Help:**
📌 *"Rewrite this grant proposal section to address funder feedback on project sustainability."*

Scenario 3: The Grant is Rejected ✖

✅ **Next Steps:**

- **Request Feedback:** Politely ask for **reviewer comments** to understand why the proposal was declined.
- **Identify Areas for Improvement:** Use feedback to refine future applications.
- **Explore Other Funding Options:** AI can assist in **finding alternative grant opportunities**.

✅ **How AI Can Help:**

✒ *"Generate a professional email requesting feedback from a funder after a grant rejection."*

✒ *"List alternative grant opportunities for a STEM education project after a funding rejection."*

Case Study: How AI Helped Improve a Resubmitted Grant Proposal

♦ **Background:** A healthcare nonprofit applied for a **$250,000 community health grant** but was rejected due to **lack of detailed outcome measures**.

♦ **How AI Helped in the Follow-Up:**

- **Crafting a Professional Feedback Request:** AI helped **generate a concise, respectful email** requesting reviewer comments.
- **Refining the Proposal Based on Feedback:** AI suggested **stronger impact metrics** and clearer project timelines.
- **Identifying Alternative Grants:** AI provided a **list of similar funding opportunities** for resubmission.

♦ **Outcome:** The nonprofit resubmitted an **improved proposal** and **secured funding from a different grant** within six months.

♦ **Key Takeaway:** Following up professionally and refining proposals based on feedback can turn rejections into future grant success.

Practical AI Prompts for Grant Follow-Up

1. Thanking the Funder After Grant Approval

✒ *"Write a thank-you letter to a funder after receiving a grant for a community outreach program."*

2. Requesting Feedback After a Grant Rejection

✒ *"Draft a professional email requesting reviewer feedback after a declined grant proposal."*

3. Resubmitting an Improved Grant Proposal

📌 *"Suggest ways to strengthen a rejected grant proposal focused on educational equity."*

4. Finding Alternative Funding Opportunities

📌 *"Identify three new funding opportunities for a nonprofit that supports at-risk youth."*

5. Providing Progress Updates to Funders

📌 *"Draft an update report to a funder highlighting the first three months of a grant-funded literacy program."*

By using AI to streamline **follow-up communications**, grant applicants can **maintain funder relationships and increase long-term funding opportunities**.

Looking Ahead

Now that we've covered **grant follow-up best practices**, the next and final section of this chapter will focus on **preparing for future grant applications**—including how AI can assist in long-term funding strategy and capacity building.

Reflection Questions:

1. How can a strong follow-up strategy help improve your grant writing success rate?
2. What follow-up actions have you taken in the past, and how could they be improved?
3. How can AI help you maintain better relationships with funders?

Section 10: Preparing for Future Grant Applications

Winning one grant is a success, but **building a sustainable funding strategy requires ongoing preparation**. Many organizations operate in **a cycle of continuous grant writing**, ensuring they have funding for current and future initiatives.

This section will explore:
- ✅ **How to build a long-term grant strategy**
- ✅ **The role of AI in tracking funding opportunities**
- ✅ **Best practices for maintaining grant application records**
- ✅ **Practical AI prompts for improving future grant writing**

Building a Sustainable Grant Writing Strategy

Instead of treating grant applications as one-time efforts, organizations should **develop a structured approach** to securing funding year after year.

Strategy	Why It's Important	AI-Enhanced Solution
1. Maintain a Grant Calendar	Helps plan ahead and avoid last-minute scrambling.	AI can **track upcoming grant deadlines** and send reminders.
2. Analyze Past Submissions	Learning from past applications improves future success.	AI can identify **patterns in successful and rejected proposals**.
3. Build a Strong Grant Template Library	Saves time by reusing well-written proposal sections.	AI can **store and modify grant proposal templates**.
4. Strengthen Relationships with Funders	Staying connected increases future funding chances.	AI can assist in **writing follow-up emails and progress reports**.
5. Stay Updated on Funding Trends	Helps identify new opportunities and changes in grant priorities.	AI can analyze **emerging trends in grant funding** and suggest adjustments.

By **adopting a proactive approach** to grant writing, organizations can **increase efficiency and maximize funding opportunities**.

How AI Can Help with Long-Term Grant Planning

AI-powered tools can assist in **automating and optimizing grant planning processes**, making it easier to manage multiple applications over time.

AI Capability	*How It Enhances Grant Strategy*
Automated Grant Discovery	AI can continuously scan for **new funding opportunities**.
Proposal Version Control	AI can store, edit, and compare **previous grant applications**.
Impact Tracking and Reporting	AI can generate **progress updates for funders** based on project data.
Content Reuse and Adaptation	AI can modify **previously successful proposals** for new applications.

Organizations that integrate AI into **long-term grant strategy development** can **save time and increase funding success rates**.

Case Study: How AI Helped a Nonprofit Build a Long-Term Grant Strategy

◆ **Background:** A nonprofit focused on youth mentorship secured a **$100,000 grant**, but needed a sustainable plan to ensure future funding.

◆ **Challenges:**

- Staff struggled with **managing multiple applications**.
- Keeping track of **deadlines and reporting requirements** was overwhelming.
- They lacked a **structured system for refining rejected proposals**.

◆ **How AI Helped:**

- **Grant Calendar Automation:** AI created a **custom grant submission timeline** with deadlines and reminders.
- **Proposal Template Optimization:** AI **refined successful proposal sections** for future applications.
- **Impact Report Assistance:** AI helped generate **quarterly reports** to keep funders engaged.

- **Outcome:** The nonprofit successfully **secured three additional grants** over the next two years, ensuring program sustainability.

- **Key Takeaway:** A long-term AI-assisted grant strategy reduces workload and increases funding opportunities.

Practical AI Prompts for Future Grant Planning

1. Tracking Grant Opportunities

📌 *"Find new grant opportunities for community-based mental health initiatives in 2025."*

2. Analyzing Past Proposal Performance

📌 *"Compare these two grant proposals and identify key differences that may have led to one being approved and the other rejected."*

3. Automating a Grant Calendar

📌 *"Create a grant submission timeline for the next 12 months based on these funding opportunities: [insert details]."*

4. Preparing Impact Reports for Funders

📌 *"Draft a six-month progress report summarizing how a grant-funded program has impacted participants."*

5. Refining Proposal Sections for Future Applications

📌 *"Rewrite the problem statement of this past grant proposal to align with a new funding opportunity."*

By using AI **to streamline future grant applications**, organizations can **stay ahead of funding needs and continuously improve their proposals**.

Final Thoughts: Mastering Grant Writing with AI

Securing grants is an **ongoing process that requires research, strategic planning, and continuous improvement**. AI is not a replacement for human expertise, but it serves as a **powerful tool** to **enhance efficiency, refine proposals, and increase funding success.**

Organizations that embrace AI-assisted grant writing will:
- ✅ **Save time** on research and proposal drafting.
- ✅ **Improve the quality** of applications through AI-powered editing and data analysis.
- ✅ **Maintain strong funder relationships** with automated follow-ups and reporting.
- ✅ **Increase their chances of securing funding** through strategic long-term planning.

By integrating AI into the **grant writing workflow**, individuals and organizations can **position themselves for ongoing success in securing funding**.

Looking Ahead to Chapter 2

Now that we've covered the **foundations of grant writing and how AI can enhance the process, Chapter 2** will dive into **"AI Tools and Techniques for Grant Writing Success"**—exploring specific AI platforms and best practices for optimizing grant applications.

Reflection Questions:

1. How can you integrate AI into your grant writing process for long-term success?
2. What challenges do you face in managing multiple grant applications?
3. How can AI help improve your organization's funding strategy over time?

Chapter 1 Summary: Key Takeaways

- ✅ Understanding different types of grants and funding sources
- ✅ How to structure a compelling, data-driven grant proposal
- ✅ Common grant writing mistakes and how AI can help avoid them
- ✅ AI-assisted strategies for refining and personalizing proposals
- ✅ How to finalize, submit, and follow up on grant applications
- ✅ Developing a sustainable, long-term AI-enhanced grant strategy

Chapter 2: AI Tools and Techniques for Grant Writing Success

Section 1: Overview of AI in Grant Writing

AI is transforming grant writing by **automating repetitive tasks, enhancing proposal quality, and optimizing research efficiency**. However, to use AI effectively, grant writers need to understand its **capabilities, limitations, and best practices**.

This section will explore:
- ✓ **How AI is revolutionizing grant writing**
- ✓ **The different types of AI tools available**
- ✓ **AI's strengths and limitations in grant writing**
- ✓ **Practical AI prompts for optimizing grant applications**

How AI is Changing Grant Writing

Traditionally, grant writing has been a **time-intensive and resource-heavy process**, requiring expertise in research, technical writing, and strategic planning. AI now offers **powerful enhancements** by:

- ✒ **Accelerating research** – AI can scan vast databases for relevant grant opportunities and background research.
- ✒ **Streamlining drafting** – AI can generate structured proposal sections based on minimal input.
- ✒ **Improving clarity and readability** – AI can refine language, remove jargon, and improve conciseness.
- ✒ **Ensuring compliance** – AI can check whether proposals meet funder requirements.
- ✒ **Enhancing budget justifications** – AI can analyze financial data and suggest clearer narratives.

By integrating AI into the grant writing workflow, individuals and organizations can **save time and improve the quality of their proposals**.

Types of AI Tools for Grant Writing

AI tools used in grant writing fall into **four main categories**, each designed to optimize different aspects of the process.

Category	Function	Example AI Tools
Grant Research & Opportunity Identification	Finds and categorizes relevant grants.	**Grants.gov, GrantStation, Instrumentl**
Proposal Drafting & Content Generation	Assists in structuring and writing proposals.	**ChatGPT, Bard, Claude, Jasper AI**
Editing & Proofreading	Improves grammar, readability, and clarity.	**Grammarly, Hemingway Editor, ProWritingAid**
Data Analysis & Budgeting	Summarizes reports, trends, and financials.	**Excel AI, OpenRefine, Tableau AI**

Each of these tools **enhances different aspects of grant writing**, making the process **more efficient and data-driven**.

AI's Strengths and Limitations in Grant Writing

While AI is a **powerful assistant**, it is **not a replacement for human expertise**. Below is a breakdown of its **strengths and limitations**:

AI Strengths	AI Limitations
Increases efficiency and reduces writing time.	May produce **generic or repetitive content** if not fine-tuned.
Enhances grammar, clarity, and structure.	Lacks **creativity and emotional depth** in storytelling.
Summarizes and organizes data effectively.	Needs **human review** for accuracy and contextual relevance.
Identifies funding opportunities based on project goals.	Cannot replace **relationship-building with funders**.

To maximize success, grant writers should **use AI as a support tool** while maintaining **human oversight and strategic decision-making**.

Case Study: AI-Powered Grant Proposal Optimization

♦ **Background:** A nonprofit organization applied for a **$500,000 environmental sustainability grant** but struggled with **writing clarity and budget justifications**.

♦ **Challenges:**

- The proposal **lacked a strong problem statement**.
- The **budget justification was too vague** for the funder's guidelines.
- The **writing was overly technical**, making it difficult to read.

♦ **How AI Helped:**

- **Drafting Support:** AI generated a **refined problem statement with supporting data**.
- **Budget Clarification:** AI structured a **clear budget justification**, aligning with funder expectations.
- **Editing & Simplification:** AI **reworded technical jargon** to make the proposal more engaging.

♦ **Outcome:** The nonprofit submitted a **polished, compelling proposal** and **secured full funding**.

♦ **Key Takeaway:** AI-powered tools can significantly improve grant proposal clarity, compliance, and impact.

Practical AI Prompts for Enhancing Grant Writing

1. Finding Grant Opportunities

📌 *"Identify upcoming education grants for K-12 schools with application deadlines in the next six months."*

2. Refining Problem Statements

📌 *"Write a problem statement for a grant proposal on expanding mental health resources in public schools, incorporating data."*

3. Improving Budget Justifications

✒ *"Generate a budget justification explaining why $100,000 is needed for program expansion."*

4. Enhancing Readability and Engagement

✒ *"Rewrite this grant proposal section to improve clarity and make it more compelling."*

5. Checking Grant Proposal Compliance

✒ *"Review this proposal against the funder's priorities and identify areas for improvement."*

By using **AI strategically**, grant writers can **increase efficiency, strengthen proposals, and improve funding success rates**.

Looking Ahead

Now that we've covered **an overview of AI's role in grant writing**, the next section will **dive deeper into specific AI-powered tools and their best applications in each stage of grant writing**.

Reflection Questions:

1. What aspects of grant writing do you find most time-consuming?
2. How could AI tools help you streamline your grant proposal process?
3. What AI tools have you already used, and how effective have they been?

Chapter 2, Section 1 Summary

✓ AI is revolutionizing grant writing by enhancing efficiency, clarity, and research capabilities.
✓ Different AI tools serve different functions, from grant research to editing and budgeting.
✓ AI has limitations—it requires human oversight, creativity, and strategic thinking.
✓ Grant writers should integrate AI to optimize, not replace, the grant writing process.

Section 2: Best AI Tools for Grant Research and Writing

Finding the right funding opportunities and crafting a compelling grant proposal requires **research, organization, and strategic writing**. AI tools can **significantly improve efficiency** in these areas by automating research, structuring content, and refining proposals.

This section will explore:
- ✓ **The best AI tools for grant research and writing**
- ✓ **How each tool enhances different stages of the grant process**
- ✓ **AI-assisted grant research strategies**
- ✓ **Practical AI prompts for grant research and writing**

AI Tools for Grant Research and Identification

Before writing a proposal, it's crucial to **identify the best funding opportunities**. AI-powered grant research tools **scan thousands of funding databases** and match grants to an organization's mission, goals, and eligibility.

AI Tool	*Function*	*Best For*
Grants.gov	Searches federal grant opportunities and provides application guidelines.	Nonprofits, education, government agencies.
GrantStation	Provides a curated list of foundation, corporate, and federal grants.	Nonprofits, small businesses, and social enterprises.
Instrumentl	Uses AI to match organizations with relevant grants and deadlines.	Long-term grant strategy and funding discovery.
OpenGrants	AI-powered search for government and private grants.	Startups, researchers, and social impact organizations.
Foundation Directory Online	Tracks private foundations and their grantmaking history.	Identifying funders for philanthropic and nonprofit projects.

By using these **AI-driven research tools**, organizations can **find the best-fit funding opportunities faster** and **avoid wasting time on misaligned grants**.

AI Tools for Grant Proposal Writing and Optimization

Once funding opportunities are identified, AI-powered writing tools help **draft, edit, and refine** grant proposals for clarity, compliance, and impact.

AI Tool	*Function*	*Best For*
ChatGPT	Generates proposal drafts, problem statements, and budget justifications.	Drafting all sections of a grant proposal.
Gemini (Google AI)	Summarizes research and enhances proposal clarity.	Background research and proposal refinement.
Claude (Anthropic AI)	Analyzes funding guidelines and refines proposal sections.	Ensuring alignment with funder priorities.
Jasper AI	Helps structure narratives and enhances persuasive writing.	Strengthening storytelling and impact statements.
Grammarly	Checks for grammar, tone, and readability issues.	Final proofreading and clarity improvement.
Hemingway Editor	Highlights overly complex sentences for simplification.	Making proposals more concise and accessible.

Using **AI writing and editing tools** ensures that grant proposals are **clear, well-structured, and aligned with funder priorities**.

How to Use AI for Grant Research and Writing

♦ **Step 1: Researching Grant Opportunities**

- Use **AI-powered databases** to identify **relevant grants**.
- Analyze past funded projects to **understand what funders prioritize**.
- Cross-check **eligibility criteria** to ensure the grant is a good fit.

♦ **Step 2: Drafting Key Proposal Sections**

- Use **ChatGPT or Jasper AI** to draft the **problem statement and objectives**.
- Structure the proposal using **AI-assisted templates**.
- Generate **SMART goals** to ensure clarity in project planning.

- ♦ **Step 3: Refining and Editing**

  - Use **Grammarly and Hemingway Editor** to simplify **complex sections**.
  - Ensure alignment with funder priorities using **Claude AI or Bard**.
  - Check for **consistency, tone, and readability** before final submission.

By combining **AI-powered research, drafting, and editing tools**, grant writers can create **stronger, more competitive proposals in less time**.

Case Study: How AI Improved Grant Research and Writing

- ♦ **Background:** A university research team needed funding for a **STEM education program** but had limited staff to conduct grant research and writing.

- ♦ **Challenges:**

  - **Finding suitable grants** took weeks of manual research.
  - The **writing process was slow**, with multiple iterations required.
  - **Ensuring compliance with funder guidelines** was time-consuming.

- ♦ **How AI Helped:**

  - **AI-powered research tools (Grants.gov & Instrumentl)** identified **four relevant STEM grants** within minutes.
  - **ChatGPT structured the proposal draft**, aligning sections with funder guidelines.
  - **Grammarly and Bard refined the language** to improve clarity and impact.

- ♦ **Outcome:** The team **submitted a competitive proposal ahead of schedule** and secured a **$300,000 grant for their STEM program**.

- ♦ **Key Takeaway:** AI tools streamlined research, improved writing quality, and ensured compliance—leading to faster, stronger proposals.

Practical AI Prompts for Grant Research and Writing

1. Finding Grant Opportunities

📌 *"Find new education grants for STEM programs with a funding range of $50,000 to $250,000."*

2. Summarizing Grant Requirements

📌 *"Summarize the eligibility criteria, deadlines, and required documents for this grant: [insert grant details]."*

3. Drafting a Problem Statement

📌 *"Write a compelling problem statement for a grant proposal addressing food insecurity in urban communities."*

4. Refining Proposal Language

📌 *"Simplify and enhance the clarity of this grant proposal section: [insert text]."*

5. Checking Proposal Alignment with Funders

📌 *"Analyze this grant proposal and suggest ways to improve alignment with [funder's name]'s priorities."*

By using **AI to optimize research and writing**, grant applicants can **reduce workload, enhance proposal quality, and increase funding success rates**.

Looking Ahead

Now that we've covered **the best AI tools for grant research and writing**, the next section will explore **how AI can optimize proposal storytelling and impact statements**—ensuring proposals are not just well-written, but also **compelling and persuasive**.

Reflection Questions:

1. What grant research challenges have you faced, and how could AI tools help?
2. Which AI writing and editing tools could improve your grant proposal process?
3. How can you integrate AI-driven research and writing into your long-term funding strategy?

Chapter 2, Section 2 Summary

✓ AI tools improve grant research by identifying funding opportunities faster.
✓ Proposal writing AI enhances clarity, compliance, and persuasiveness.
✓ Using AI in research and writing saves time and increases funding success.
✓ Combining multiple AI tools maximizes proposal quality and efficiency.

Section 3: Using AI for Storytelling and Impact in Grant Proposals

A well-written grant proposal is more than just facts and figures—it must **tell a compelling story** that resonates with funders. Strong storytelling can **evoke emotion, highlight urgency, and create a persuasive case** for funding. AI can assist in structuring narratives, refining messaging, and enhancing the emotional appeal of grant proposals.

This section will explore:
✓ **Why storytelling is crucial in grant proposals**
✓ **How AI can help craft impactful narratives**
✓ **Best practices for writing compelling impact statements**
✓ **Practical AI prompts for enhancing storytelling in grants**

Why Storytelling is Crucial in Grant Proposals

Funders receive **hundreds, if not thousands, of applications**—many of which contain similar statistics and project descriptions. A strong, **human-centered story** can:

★ **Make the proposal memorable** – Funders are more likely to remember stories than raw data.
★ **Evoke emotion and urgency** – Stories create a sense of **why the funding matters**.
★ **Demonstrate real-world impact** – Case studies and testimonials **bring data to life**.
★ **Showcase the organization's mission** – A compelling narrative reflects the **passion behind the project**.

By incorporating **narrative elements and real-world impact**, grant proposals become **more persuasive and engaging**.

How AI Can Enhance Storytelling in Grant Proposals

AI can **support storytelling** by helping craft narratives, structure personal stories, and refine messaging for clarity and emotional impact.

AI Capability	How It Enhances Storytelling
Generating Narrative Structures	AI can suggest **story arcs** to make proposals more compelling.
Personalizing Case Studies	AI can help structure **individual success stories** to highlight impact.
Refining Emotional Appeals	AI can enhance language to **increase engagement and relatability**.
Improving Clarity and Flow	AI can ensure **stories are concise and powerful** without unnecessary complexity.

While AI can **help shape stories**, human input is **essential for authenticity and depth**.

Best Practices for Writing Compelling Impact Statements

An **impact statement** is one of the most crucial parts of a grant proposal—it tells funders **why their support will make a difference**. Below are key best practices:

1. Start with a Powerful Hook

◆ **Example:** *"Imagine a classroom where students struggle to read because they don't have access to books. Now imagine a program that provides those books and changes lives forever."*

✓ **AI Tip:** Use AI to **generate multiple opening lines** and select the most engaging one.
➤ **AI Prompt:** *"Write an engaging opening sentence for a grant proposal on early childhood literacy."*

---

2. Use Real Stories and Testimonials

◆ **Example:** Instead of saying *"This program improves literacy rates,"* say:
"Maria, a 10-year-old student, started the school year unable to read a full paragraph. After six months in our literacy program, she confidently reads aloud in class and writes her own short stories."

- ✅ **AI Tip:** AI can **structure personal stories**, but ensure **authenticity by adding real details**.
- 📌 **AI Prompt:** *"Create a success story about a student who benefited from a school mentorship program."*

---

3. Show Data-Driven Impact

- ◆ **Example:** *"In the last two years, our program has increased high school graduation rates by 30%."*

- ✅ **AI Tip:** AI can **generate concise data summaries** to support impact statements.
- 📌 **AI Prompt:** *"Summarize key impact data for a workforce development program improving job placement rates."*

---

4. Create a Vision for the Future

- ◆ **Example:** *"With your support, we can expand this program to reach 500 more students, ensuring every child has access to quality education."*

- ✅ **AI Tip:** AI can help craft **forward-looking, action-driven conclusions**.
- 📌 **AI Prompt:** *"Write a compelling conclusion for a grant proposal seeking funding for a community health initiative."*

Case Study: How AI Helped Strengthen Storytelling in a Grant Proposal

- ◆ **Background:** A nonprofit applied for a **$150,000 grant** to expand a **homeless outreach program** but struggled to make its impact statement compelling.

- ◆ **Challenges:**

  - The proposal **lacked a personal, emotional connection**.
  - The **impact data was buried in technical jargon**.
  - The **funders had multiple similar applications**, making differentiation critical.

- ◆ **How AI Helped:**

  - **Generating Narrative Options:** AI suggested **multiple opening hooks**, helping refine the most engaging one.

- **Structuring Personal Stories:** AI assisted in framing **a compelling success story** from a program participant.
- **Refining the Impact Statement:** AI helped **simplify complex data** into **clear, persuasive messaging**.

♦ **Outcome:** The improved proposal **stood out from competitors** and secured full funding.

♦ **Key Takeaway:** AI can refine and structure impact-driven storytelling, but human oversight ensures authenticity and depth.

Practical AI Prompts for Enhancing Storytelling and Impact

1. Crafting a Compelling Hook

📌 *"Generate an engaging opening line for a grant proposal addressing food insecurity."*

2. Creating a Success Story

📌 *"Write a success story about a student who benefited from a tutoring program, incorporating real-world impact."*

3. Refining an Impact Statement

📌 *"Rewrite this impact statement to make it more persuasive and emotionally engaging: [insert text]."*

4. Strengthening Data Storytelling

📌 *"Summarize these program results in a compelling and digestible way: [insert data]."*

5. Writing a Future-Focused Conclusion

📌 *"Craft a vision-driven closing statement for a grant proposal on expanding access to STEM education."*

By using **AI for storytelling and impact enhancement**, grant writers can **transform proposals from informational documents into compelling, persuasive narratives**.

Looking Ahead

Now that we've covered **how to use AI for storytelling and impact**, the next section will explore **how AI can optimize grant budgets and financial justifications**—a critical component of securing funding.

Reflection Questions:

1. How can storytelling make your grant proposals more compelling?
2. What elements of your impact statements could be improved using AI?
3. How can you balance AI-generated storytelling with authenticity in grant writing?

Chapter 2, Section 3 Summary

✓ Storytelling makes grant proposals more memorable and persuasive.
✓ AI can help structure narratives, but human oversight ensures authenticity.
✓ Impact statements should combine personal stories, data, and a vision for the future.
✓ Using AI-generated prompts can improve clarity, engagement, and emotional appeal.

Section 4: Optimizing Grant Budgets and Financial Justifications with AI

A well-structured budget is one of the most critical components of a grant proposal. Funders need to see **how the requested funds will be used, why they are necessary, and how they align with the project's goals**. A clear and well-justified budget can significantly improve the likelihood of securing funding.

This section will explore:
✓ **Why grant budgets and financial justifications matter**
✓ **Common budgeting mistakes and how to avoid them**
✓ **How AI can assist in budget planning and justification**
✓ **Practical AI prompts for optimizing grant budgets**

Why Budgets and Financial Justifications Matter in Grant Proposals

A budget tells **the financial story** of a grant proposal. It answers the following questions for funders:

- ✒ **How much funding is needed?** – Specifies the exact amount requested.
- ✒ **Where will the money go?** – Breaks down the allocation of funds.
- ✒ **Why are these expenses necessary?** – Provides a rationale for each budget item.
- ✒ **How does the budget align with project goals?** – Demonstrates financial responsibility and impact.

A **clear and well-documented budget** reassures funders that the grant will be managed efficiently and used for its intended purpose.

Common Budgeting Mistakes and How to Avoid Them

Mistake	Why It's a Problem	AI-Enhanced Solution
1. Lack of Detail	Funders need itemized costs to understand spending priorities.	AI can generate **detailed budget templates** and justifications.
2. Inconsistent Budget & Proposal Narrative	If the budget doesn't align with the proposal's objectives, it raises red flags.	AI can cross-check budget allocations against project goals.
3. Forgetting Indirect Costs	Some grants allow administrative or overhead expenses, but applicants often omit them.	AI can suggest **allowable indirect costs** based on funder guidelines.
4. Unrealistic Cost Estimates	Costs that are too high or too low can make funders skeptical.	AI can help research **industry-standard cost estimates**.
5. Missing Matching Funds or In-Kind Contributions	Many grants require cost-sharing, which some applicants overlook.	AI can identify **matching fund requirements** and suggest in-kind contributions.

By **addressing these common budgeting errors**, applicants can **improve funder confidence** in their financial planning.

How AI Can Assist in Budget Planning and Justification

AI-powered tools can **simplify, refine, and optimize** the budget creation process.

AI Function	How It Enhances Budgeting
Budget Template Generation	AI can create structured budget formats based on industry best practices.
Cost Research and Estimation	AI can analyze standard costs for salaries, supplies, and operational expenses.
Expense Justification Writing	AI can draft **concise, compelling budget narratives**.
Alignment Verification	AI can ensure that **budget categories align with the grant's objectives**.

By leveraging **AI-assisted budgeting tools**, grant writers can create **accurate, transparent, and persuasive financial justifications**.

Best Practices for Writing a Persuasive Budget Justification

A budget justification **explains why each expense is necessary** and how it contributes to the project's success. Follow these best practices:

1. Clearly Define Each Budget Category

♦ **Example:** Instead of writing *"Personnel: $50,000"*, write:
"A project coordinator will oversee daily operations, ensuring program success and compliance. The requested $50,000 will cover salary and benefits for a full-time role."

✓ **AI Tip:** AI can generate detailed justifications for budget categories.
★ **AI Prompt:** *"Write a budget justification for hiring a full-time project manager at $50,000 per year."*

---

2. Use Realistic and Justifiable Costs

♦ **Example:** Instead of *"Supplies: $20,000"*, write:
"The budget includes $20,000 for classroom technology, including 30 Chromebooks ($500 each) to support digital literacy programs."

✅ **AI Tip:** AI can break down expenses into funder-friendly justifications.
✈ **AI Prompt:** *"Create a cost breakdown for a $20,000 budget request covering classroom technology."*

---

3. Align the Budget with Project Goals

♦ **Example:** If the project focuses on **STEM education**, show how each cost supports that goal.

✅ **AI Tip:** AI can cross-check budget narratives against proposal objectives.
✈ **AI Prompt:** *"Ensure this budget aligns with the project objectives outlined in the proposal."*

---

4. Justify Indirect Costs and Administrative Expenses

♦ **Example:** *"The budget includes 10% in indirect costs ($10,000) to cover rent, utilities, and administrative support, ensuring smooth project implementation."*

✅ **AI Tip:** AI can suggest indirect cost justifications based on funder guidelines.
✈ **AI Prompt:** *"Write a budget justification explaining indirect costs at 10% of the total request."*

Case Study: How AI Helped Improve a Grant Budget Justification

♦ **Background:** A small business applied for a **$100,000 entrepreneurship grant** but was rejected due to an **unclear budget justification**.

♦ **Challenges:**

- The **budget lacked detailed explanations** for key expenses.
- The **funders questioned the necessity of certain costs**.
- The justification **did not align well with the grant's mission**.

♦ **How AI Helped:**

- **Clarifying Expenses:** AI-generated **clear justifications** for each budget category.
- **Ensuring Alignment:** AI **rewrote cost explanations** to match the proposal's goals.
- **Improving Presentation:** AI helped format the budget **in an easy-to-read structure**.

- ◆ **Outcome:** The business **resubmitted the improved budget justification and secured full funding**.

- ◆ **Key Takeaway:** A well-justified, AI-assisted budget can strengthen a grant proposal and increase funding success.

Practical AI Prompts for Grant Budget Optimization

1. Structuring a Budget Template

📌 *"Generate a standard grant budget template for a nonprofit applying for a community development grant."*

2. Creating a Justification for Personnel Costs

📌 *"Write a budget justification for a $60,000 program director salary, including rationale for the role."*

3. Breaking Down Equipment or Supply Costs

📌 *"Provide a cost breakdown and justification for purchasing 20 laptops for an educational technology program."*

4. Explaining Indirect Costs

📌 *"Create a justification for including 10% indirect costs in a federal grant proposal."*

5. Checking Budget Alignment with Proposal Objectives

📌 *"Review this budget and ensure it aligns with the project goals outlined in the proposal."*

By using **AI-driven budget planning and justification tools**, grant writers can **increase transparency, improve funder confidence, and enhance proposal credibility**.

Looking Ahead

Now that we've covered **how to optimize grant budgets and financial justifications**, the next section will explore **how AI can enhance collaboration and teamwork in grant writing**—helping teams streamline workflow and manage applications efficiently.

Reflection Questions:

1. How can AI help improve the clarity and alignment of your grant budget?
2. What budget challenges have you faced in past proposals, and how could AI assist?
3. How can AI-driven cost analysis improve funder confidence in your proposals?

Chapter 2, Section 4 Summary

✅ **A strong budget tells the financial story of a grant proposal.**
✅ **Common budgeting mistakes—such as lack of detail and misalignment—can be avoided using AI.**
✅ **AI-powered tools improve budget structuring, justification, and cost estimation.**
✅ **Well-justified budgets increase funder confidence and grant approval chances.**

Section 5: Enhancing Collaboration and Workflow in Grant Writing with AI

Grant writing is rarely a solo effort—most applications require **collaboration between teams, stakeholders, and subject matter experts**. AI can play a crucial role in improving **workflow efficiency, document organization, and real-time collaboration** among team members.

This section will explore:
✅ **How AI improves collaboration in grant writing**
✅ **AI tools for streamlining workflow and document management**
✅ **Best practices for team-based AI-assisted grant writing**
✅ **Practical AI prompts for optimizing team collaboration**

How AI Enhances Collaboration in Grant Writing

When multiple team members contribute to a grant application, challenges can arise, such as **version control issues, communication gaps, and inconsistent writing styles**. AI-driven collaboration tools help by:

- ✒ **Automating document organization** – AI ensures consistency across multiple drafts.
- ✒ **Providing real-time editing and feedback** – AI can highlight clarity issues and suggest improvements.
- ✒ **Improving team coordination** – AI can assign tasks, set deadlines, and track progress.
- ✒ **Streamlining revision cycles** – AI-assisted editing tools help align different writing styles into a cohesive voice.

By **integrating AI into the grant writing workflow**, teams can **work more efficiently, reduce errors, and enhance proposal quality**.

AI Tools for Streamlining Grant Writing Collaboration

AI-powered platforms improve team coordination by enabling **real-time editing, feedback, and organization**.

AI Tool	Function	Best For
Google Docs + AI Writing Add-ons	Enables real-time editing, AI-powered suggestions, and team comments.	Grant writing teams working on shared proposals.
Notion AI	Organizes notes, tracks deadlines, and generates structured content.	Teams managing multiple grant applications.
Trello + AI Automation	Helps track grant timelines and assign writing tasks.	Managing grant project workflow.
ChatGPT (Team Mode)	Provides AI-assisted writing and content refinement.	Teams needing AI-generated drafts and revisions.
Microsoft Copilot (Word + Excel)	Enhances writing clarity and automates budget calculations.	Organizations using Microsoft-based grant writing.

By **leveraging AI-driven collaboration tools**, teams can streamline **grant proposal development, tracking, and submission processes**.

Best Practices for Team-Based AI-Assisted Grant Writing

Collaboration is most effective when teams establish **clear roles and workflows** for grant writing. Below are key best practices:

1. Define Roles and Responsibilities

Ensure each team member knows their specific role, such as:
- **Lead Writer** – Oversees overall structure and proposal cohesion.
- **Researcher** – Gathers background data and funding requirements.
- **Budget Analyst** – Develops and justifies financial details.
- **Editor/Reviewer** – Checks for clarity, alignment, and compliance.

✅ **AI Tip:** AI can suggest **task assignments** based on team expertise.
📌 **AI Prompt:** *"Generate a task breakdown for a grant writing team applying for an education grant."*

---

2. Use AI to Ensure Consistency in Writing Style

When multiple people contribute to a grant proposal, maintaining a **unified tone and voice** is essential.

✅ **AI Tip:** AI can **standardize tone and style** across different sections.
📌 **AI Prompt:** *"Rewrite this proposal section to match a professional, persuasive, and engaging tone."*

---

3. Automate Project Management with AI

- **Example:** A nonprofit managing multiple grants can use **AI-powered Trello or Notion dashboards** to:
✅ Track **application deadlines**
✅ Assign **proposal sections to team members**
✅ Monitor **revision progress**

✅ **AI Tip:** AI can generate structured task lists and reminders.
📌 **AI Prompt:** *"Create a project timeline for completing a federal grant application over the next eight weeks."*

4. Enable AI-Assisted Feedback and Revisions

- **Example:** Before submission, AI-powered tools like **Grammarly, ChatGPT, and Copilot** can:
  - ✓ Check for **grammar and clarity**
  - ✓ Ensure **alignment with funder priorities**
  - ✓ Identify **gaps in justification**

- ✓ **AI Tip:** AI can conduct **automated proposal reviews** and highlight weak areas.
- ✦ **AI Prompt:** *"Analyze this grant proposal draft and provide feedback on clarity, alignment, and persuasiveness."*

---

5. Create AI-Generated Meeting Summaries and Action Items

- **Example:** AI tools like **Otter.ai or Notion AI** can:
  - ✓ Transcribe grant team meetings
  - ✓ Summarize key discussion points
  - ✓ Generate action items

- ✓ **AI Tip:** AI can provide **concise meeting notes and next steps**.
- ✦ **AI Prompt:** *"Summarize the key action items from this grant team meeting transcript."*

Case Study: How AI Improved Team Collaboration in Grant Writing

- **Background:** A school district applied for a **$500,000 STEM education grant** but faced challenges in coordinating across multiple departments.

- **Challenges:**

  - Disjointed writing styles from different team members.
  - Delays in editing and finalizing key sections.
  - Lack of clear task ownership for budgeting and research.

- **How AI Helped:**

  - **Streamlining Content Review:** ChatGPT aligned **tone and writing style** across different sections.
  - **Task Organization:** Trello AI automated **task assignments and deadlines**.

- **Budget Refinement:** Microsoft Copilot structured **financial details and justifications**.

♦ **Outcome:** The team **completed the grant proposal ahead of schedule** and successfully secured funding.

♦ **Key Takeaway:** AI-driven collaboration tools improve workflow efficiency and create cohesive, high-quality grant applications.

Practical AI Prompts for Optimizing Team Collaboration in Grant Writing

1. Assigning Roles and Responsibilities

📌 *"Outline the key responsibilities for a team writing a $100,000 community health grant proposal."*

2. Ensuring Writing Consistency

📌 *"Rewrite this grant proposal section to ensure it matches the overall proposal tone and style."*

3. Automating Task Assignments

📌 *"Generate a weekly task schedule for a team preparing a grant application due in two months."*

4. AI-Assisted Proposal Review

📌 *"Analyze this proposal and suggest areas for improvement in clarity, alignment, and impact."*

5. Generating Meeting Summaries and Next Steps

📌 *"Summarize the key action items from this team discussion on the upcoming grant proposal."*

By **incorporating AI tools into team collaboration**, organizations can **enhance efficiency, streamline workflows, and improve the quality of their grant applications.**

Looking Ahead

Now that we've covered **how AI enhances collaboration in grant writing**, the next section will focus on **how AI can help refine and optimize final grant proposals before submission**—ensuring they meet funder expectations and stand out.

Reflection Questions:

1. How can AI improve collaboration and efficiency in your grant writing team?
2. What AI tools could help streamline workflow and communication?
3. How can AI-driven feedback improve proposal clarity and alignment before submission?

Chapter 2, Section 5 Summary

✓ **AI enhances grant writing collaboration by improving workflow efficiency.**
✓ **AI tools like Google Docs, Trello, and Notion AI help track progress and assignments.**
✓ **AI ensures consistency in writing style across team-contributed sections.**
✓ **Automated AI reviews help identify clarity, alignment, and impact improvements.**

Section 6: AI-Assisted Proposal Finalization and Submission Best Practices

Finalizing and submitting a grant proposal requires **thorough review, compliance checks, and strategic submission planning**. Even the most well-written proposals can be rejected if they fail to meet funder requirements or contain overlooked errors. AI can assist in **polishing proposals, ensuring compliance, and optimizing submission timing**.

This section will explore:
✓ **The final steps before submitting a grant proposal**
✓ **How AI enhances proofreading, compliance, and document formatting**
✓ **Best practices for a seamless submission process**
✓ **Practical AI prompts for finalizing and submitting proposals**

The Final Steps Before Submitting a Grant Proposal

Before submitting a proposal, **perform a final review** to ensure clarity, compliance, and completeness.

Final Review Step	Why It's Important	AI-Assisted Solution
1. Proofread for Grammar, Clarity, and Tone	Typos, unclear phrasing, or inconsistent tone can reduce credibility.	AI tools like **Grammarly and Hemingway Editor** refine readability.
2. Ensure Proposal Alignment with Funders' Priorities	Proposals should explicitly align with funder goals.	AI can analyze the proposal against funder guidelines and suggest refinements.
3. Verify Compliance with Submission Requirements	Incorrect formatting, missing attachments, or exceeding word limits can result in rejection.	AI can cross-check document structure against funder requirements.
4. Double-Check Budget Justifications	Financial inconsistencies or vague cost descriptions weaken proposals.	AI can generate **clear budget narratives** and verify calculations.
5. Optimize Proposal Structure for Readability	Poor organization can make key points hard to find.	AI can suggest improved **headings, bullet points, and summaries**.
6. Conduct a Final Peer Review	External feedback improves proposal quality.	AI can **highlight unclear sections and suggest refinements**.

By **completing these final review steps**, applicants can ensure that their proposal is **polished, funder-ready, and free of critical errors**.

How AI Enhances Proofreading, Compliance, and Document Formatting

AI tools improve the **finalization process** by automating quality checks and ensuring compliance with funder expectations.

AI Tool	Function	Best For
Grammarly	Checks grammar, tone, and clarity.	Final proofreading and readability improvement.
Hemingway Editor	Highlights overly complex sentences and improves readability.	Ensuring proposals are clear and concise.
ChatGPT/Bard	Suggests structure, wording, and alignment improvements.	Refining impact statements and narrative flow.
Claude AI	Checks for compliance with funder priorities.	Ensuring the proposal meets funder expectations.
Microsoft Word Copilot	Automates formatting and structure consistency.	Ensuring professional document presentation.

Using **AI-powered finalization tools**, applicants can create **clear, persuasive, and error-free proposals**.

Best Practices for a Seamless Submission Process

Submitting a grant proposal **on time and correctly formatted** increases its chances of success. Follow these best practices:

1. Submit Early to Avoid Last-Minute Issues

✓ Plan to submit **at least 48 hours before the deadline** to allow time for unexpected technical issues.

★ **AI Prompt:** *"Generate a submission checklist for a federal grant application with a deadline in one week."*

2. Verify All Required Attachments Are Included

✓ Most funders require **letters of support, budgets, and supplemental documents**. Ensure nothing is missing.

📌 **AI Prompt:** *"Create a checklist of common supporting documents required for an education grant application."*

---

3. Double-Check Formatting Requirements

✓ Follow **page limits, font guidelines, and file format instructions**.

📌 **AI Prompt:** *"Check this grant proposal for adherence to formatting guidelines and suggest corrections."*

---

4. Ensure Digital Submission Confirmation

✓ If submitting online, verify that the **proposal was received and no errors occurred during upload**.

📌 **AI Prompt:** *"Draft a professional email confirming the successful submission of a grant proposal to [funder name]."*

---

5. Keep a Copy of the Submitted Proposal for Future Reference

✓ Store a **finalized version** along with submission receipts in a secure location for record-keeping.

📌 **AI Prompt:** *"Organize a document storage system for tracking past and current grant applications."*

Case Study: How AI Helped Perfect a Grant Proposal Before Submission

♦ **Background:** A nonprofit applied for a **$250,000 health initiative grant** but needed last-minute refinements before submission.

♦ **Challenges:**

- The **narrative lacked clarity** in the impact section.
- The **budget justification had vague cost explanations**.
- The **submission portal required specific formatting adjustments**.

♦ **How AI Helped:**

- **ChatGPT revised the impact statement** to strengthen the proposal's emotional appeal.
- **Microsoft Copilot reformatted tables and figures** for compliance.
- **Grammarly performed a final proofreading check**, ensuring grammatical accuracy.

♦ **Outcome:** The proposal was **submitted on time and met all funder requirements**, leading to **a successful funding award**.

♦ **Key Takeaway:** AI-assisted finalization helps eliminate errors, enhance readability, and improve compliance, increasing funding success.

Practical AI Prompts for Finalizing and Submitting Grant Proposals

1. Checking for Clarity and Readability

✦ *"Analyze this grant proposal and suggest edits to improve clarity, readability, and engagement."*

2. Verifying Alignment with Funder Priorities

✦ *"Compare this proposal with the stated priorities of [funder's name] and suggest ways to improve alignment."*

3. Formatting and Compliance Review

📌 *"Check if this document meets the formatting and structural requirements of a federal grant submission."*

4. Creating a Submission Checklist

📌 *"Generate a step-by-step submission checklist for an upcoming grant application."*

5. Writing a Submission Confirmation Email

📌 *"Draft a professional email to confirm the successful submission of a grant proposal."*

By using **AI for final review and submission planning**, grant applicants can **eliminate errors, ensure compliance, and present a polished proposal that stands out to funders**.

Looking Ahead

Now that we've covered **how AI can optimize finalizing and submitting grant proposals**, the next section will focus on **how AI can be used for post-submission follow-ups, reporting, and future grant planning**.

Reflection Questions:

1. How can AI help you ensure grant compliance before submission?
2. What are the most common last-minute challenges in finalizing a proposal, and how could AI assist?
3. How can AI-driven quality checks improve the professionalism of your grant applications?

Chapter 2, Section 6 Summary

✓ **Finalizing a grant proposal requires compliance, proofreading, and strategic submission planning.**
✓ **AI tools enhance readability, budget accuracy, and formatting consistency.**
✓ **Submitting early, verifying attachments, and following funder guidelines improves approval chances.**
✓ **AI-generated checklists, edits, and compliance reviews streamline the finalization process.**

Section 7: AI for Post-Submission Follow-Ups, Reporting, and Future Grant Planning

Winning a grant is not the final step in the funding process—effective **post-submission follow-ups, impact reporting, and future planning** are crucial for maintaining funder relationships and securing ongoing support. AI can assist in **automating follow-up communications, generating progress reports, and refining future grant strategies**.

This section will explore:
✅ **Best practices for post-submission follow-ups**
✅ **How AI can automate reporting and impact tracking**
✅ **Strategies for future grant planning using AI**
✅ **Practical AI prompts for follow-up, reporting, and strategy development**

Best Practices for Post-Submission Follow-Ups

Whether a proposal is **approved, rejected, or under review**, **proactive follow-up** can strengthen relationships with funders and improve future applications.

Follow-Up Scenario	Recommended Actions	AI-Enhanced Solution
1. The Grant is Awarded 🎉	Send a thank-you letter, confirm funding details, and begin project implementation.	AI can generate **thank-you emails and implementation timelines**.
2. The Funder Requests Modifications ✍	Address requested changes, clarify funder feedback, and resubmit.	AI can assist in **rewriting sections based on feedback**.
3. The Grant is Rejected ✖	Request feedback, analyze proposal weaknesses, and explore alternative funding options.	AI can summarize reviewer comments and suggest **resubmission improvements**.
4. Awaiting a Decision ⌛	Send a follow-up email to check on the proposal's status after the review period.	AI can generate **polite status-check emails**.

By using **AI-generated follow-up strategies**, grant writers can **maintain funder relationships and improve future applications**.

How AI Can Automate Grant Reporting and Impact Tracking

Once a grant is awarded, **progress reports, financial tracking, and impact measurement** become essential. AI can **automate and optimize reporting** by:

📌 **Generating structured progress reports** – AI summarizes project milestones and financial updates.
📌 **Tracking key performance indicators (KPIs)** – AI analyzes program data to measure success.
📌 **Simplifying complex financial reporting** – AI formats and organizes financial statements for funders.
📌 **Creating funder-friendly data visualizations** – AI generates charts, graphs, and dashboards for impact reports.

Using **AI-powered reporting tools**, grant recipients can **streamline compliance and demonstrate accountability** to funders.

Strategies for Future Grant Planning Using AI

To maintain long-term funding success, organizations should integrate **AI-driven planning strategies** into their grant processes.

Future Planning Strategy	AI-Enhanced Approach
1. Maintaining a Grant Calendar 📅	AI can track **funding cycles and deadlines** to ensure timely applications.
2. Analyzing Past Grant Performance 📊	AI can compare **successful vs. rejected proposals** to identify improvement areas.
3. Identifying New Funding Opportunities 🔍	AI can scan **grant databases and funder trends** for upcoming opportunities.
4. Refining Proposal Templates 📝	AI can generate **customized templates based on past successful applications**.
5. Strengthening Fundraising Strategy 💡	AI can suggest **alternative funding sources** and grant diversification tactics.

By integrating AI into **long-term grant planning**, organizations can **increase efficiency, secure more funding, and refine future applications**.

Case Study: How AI Helped Optimize Post-Submission Grant Reporting and Planning

♦ **Background:** A nonprofit organization received a **$500,000 workforce development grant** but struggled with **reporting deadlines and future funding strategies**.

♦ **Challenges:**

- **Manual reporting was time-consuming and lacked structure**.
- The team needed **data-driven insights for future grant applications**.
- They lacked a **systematic approach to tracking funder relationships**.

♦ **How AI Helped:**

- **Automated Reporting:** AI-generated **quarterly progress reports** summarizing project impact.
- **Data Analysis for Future Grants:** AI **compared past successful proposals** to refine future applications.
- **Grant Calendar Automation:** AI tracked **upcoming renewal deadlines** and suggested **new funding sources**.

♦ **Outcome:** The nonprofit streamlined **reporting, identified new funding opportunities, and improved grant management efficiency**.

♦ **Key Takeaway:** AI-driven post-submission strategies enhance compliance, improve funder relations, and support long-term sustainability.

Practical AI Prompts for Follow-Up, Reporting, and Future Grant Planning

1. Writing a Grant Award Thank-You Email

📌 *"Draft a professional thank-you email to a funder after receiving a grant award."*

2. Requesting Feedback After a Grant Rejection

📌 *"Write a polite email requesting reviewer feedback on a declined grant proposal."*

3. Generating a Progress Report for Funders

✒ *"Create a six-month progress report summarizing key achievements and financial updates for a grant-funded STEM program."*

4. Identifying Alternative Funding Sources

✒ *"Find new grant opportunities for a nonprofit focused on youth mentorship programs."*

5. Automating a Grant Submission Calendar

✒ *"Generate a 12-month grant submission timeline based on these upcoming deadlines: [insert details]."*

By using **AI to optimize follow-ups, reporting, and strategic planning**, grant recipients can **maintain funder relationships, track impact effectively, and secure future funding opportunities**.

Looking Ahead

Now that we've covered **how AI enhances post-submission follow-ups and reporting**, the next and final section of Chapter 2 will focus on **emerging trends and the future of AI in grant writing**—helping organizations stay ahead in the evolving funding landscape.

Reflection Questions:

1. How can AI help automate your organization's grant reporting process?
2. What strategies can you use to strengthen funder relationships after submission?
3. How can AI-driven insights improve your long-term grant planning and funding strategy?

Chapter 2, Section 7 Summary

✓ Following up after submission strengthens funder relationships and improves future applications.
✓ **AI automates reporting, financial tracking, and impact measurement for funders.**
✓ **Strategic AI-driven grant planning increases funding success over time.**
✓ Using AI-generated follow-ups and reporting improves efficiency and compliance.

Section 8: The Future of AI in Grant Writing – Emerging Trends and Innovations

As AI technology continues to evolve, its role in **grant writing and funding acquisition** is expanding rapidly. Organizations that adopt AI-powered tools and **stay ahead of emerging trends** will have a competitive advantage in securing funding.

This section will explore:
- ✅ **Current and emerging AI trends in grant writing**
- ✅ **Innovative AI applications for funding acquisition**
- ✅ **Ethical considerations and responsible AI use in grants**
- ✅ **Practical AI prompts for staying ahead in grant writing innovation**

Emerging AI Trends in Grant Writing

As AI continues to develop, the following trends are shaping the future of grant writing:

Trend	What It Means for Grant Writers
1. AI-Powered Grant Search and Matching	AI tools will become more accurate in identifying **funding opportunities based on project goals and past success rates**.
2. Automated Proposal Drafting and Customization	AI will generate **more personalized grant proposals** that align with funder priorities using deep learning and historical data.
3. AI-Enhanced Funder Relationship Management	AI-powered CRMs will help organizations track funder interactions and recommend **best times for follow-ups and renewal requests**.
4. Advanced Predictive Analytics for Funding Success	AI will analyze **past proposal performance** to predict which grants an organization is most likely to win.
5. AI for Compliance and Risk Assessment	AI will assist in ensuring that grant applications meet **all legal, regulatory, and compliance requirements** before submission.

By integrating these **AI-driven innovations**, organizations can **improve efficiency, increase funding success rates, and strengthen funder relationships**.

Innovative AI Applications for Grant Writing and Funding Acquisition

AI is now being applied in **new and creative ways** to streamline grant writing and funding management.

AI Innovation	How It Enhances Grant Writing
AI-Powered Chatbots	Can answer **frequently asked questions** about grants, helping applicants navigate complex requirements.
Voice-to-Text AI for Grant Writing	Allows grant writers to **dictate proposals** for faster drafting.
AI-Generated Infographics & Data Visualizations	Converts impact data into **engaging charts and visuals** for funders.
Blockchain-Integrated AI for Grant Compliance	Ensures transparency in **funding allocation and reporting** through immutable records.
Multilingual AI Translation for Global Grants	Helps organizations **apply for international funding** by translating proposals accurately.

By leveraging these **AI-driven innovations**, grant writers can create **more engaging, accessible, and funder-friendly proposals**.

Ethical Considerations and Responsible AI Use in Grant Writing

While AI provides significant benefits, ethical considerations must be taken into account to ensure **fair, transparent, and responsible** use in grant writing.

Ethical Consideration	Why It Matters	Best Practices
1. Transparency in AI-Generated Content	Funders value authenticity—AI-generated proposals should be reviewed for accuracy.	Clearly indicate when AI is used and ensure final edits reflect **human oversight**.
2. Data Privacy & Security	Sensitive grant data should be protected from unauthorized access.	Use **secure AI platforms** and follow **data protection policies**.
3. Avoiding Bias in AI-Generated Content	AI models can reflect bias from their training data.	Review AI-generated proposals for **equity and inclusivity** in language and recommendations.
4. Maintaining Human Involvement in Grant Writing	AI should assist, not replace, human expertise.	Use AI for **enhancements**, but ensure proposals reflect **authentic organizational values**.

By following these **ethical best practices**, organizations can use AI **responsibly and effectively** in grant writing.

Case Study: How AI-Powered Innovations Transformed Grant Writing for a Nonprofit

◆ **Background:** A nonprofit focused on community health wanted to apply for multiple grants but faced **time constraints and staff limitations**.

◆ **Challenges:**

- **Grant research was time-intensive**, limiting the number of applications.
- **Proposal writing required extensive customization** for different funders.
- **Tracking funder relationships** across multiple grants was difficult.

♦ **How AI Helped:**

- **AI-Driven Grant Matching**: AI identified **five high-probability grant opportunities**.
- **Automated Proposal Customization**: AI adjusted **proposal language and objectives** to match each funder's priorities.
- **Predictive Analytics for Success**: AI analyzed **past grant performance** to refine the strongest funding requests.

♦ **Outcome:** The nonprofit **secured three new grants** and streamlined its funding strategy with AI-powered insights.

♦ **Key Takeaway:** AI-driven grant writing innovations save time, increase efficiency, and improve funding success rates.

Practical AI Prompts for Staying Ahead in Grant Writing Innovation

1. Finding AI-Optimized Grant Opportunities

📌 *"Identify upcoming grants for environmental nonprofits that align with sustainability goals."*

2. Automating Funder Relationship Management

📌 *"Generate a funder engagement strategy based on past interactions and grant renewal opportunities."*

3. Predicting Grant Success Likelihood

📌 *"Analyze these past five grant applications and predict which future grants are most likely to be awarded."*

4. Enhancing Proposal Presentation with AI-Generated Visuals

📌 *"Create a data visualization highlighting the impact of a community education program."*

5. Ensuring Ethical AI Use in Grant Writing

📌 *"Review this AI-generated grant proposal for potential biases and suggest edits to enhance inclusivity."*

By staying ahead of **AI trends and best practices**, grant writers can ensure they **maximize funding opportunities while maintaining ethical and responsible AI use**.

Looking Ahead

Now that we've covered **the future of AI in grant writing**, the next chapter will explore **how to implement AI-driven grant writing strategies for different industries**—including education, healthcare, nonprofits, and businesses.

Reflection Questions:

1. What AI innovations could you integrate into your current grant writing process?
2. How can AI help you predict grant success and refine future applications?
3. What ethical considerations should your organization follow when using AI for grant writing?

Chapter 2, Section 8 Summary

✓ AI-powered innovations are transforming grant writing, from predictive analytics to automated proposal customization.
✓ Emerging AI trends include funder relationship management, compliance automation, and multilingual proposal translation.
✓ Ethical AI use requires transparency, data security, and human oversight.
✓ Staying ahead in AI-driven grant writing ensures long-term funding success.

Chapter 3: Implementing AI-Driven Grant Writing Strategies for Different Industries

Section 1: How AI Adapts to Industry-Specific Grant Writing Needs

Grant writing varies significantly depending on the industry. While the **core principles of grant writing remain the same**, different industries have unique **funding priorities, compliance requirements, and evaluation metrics**. AI can help tailor grant proposals to specific industry expectations, ensuring **higher alignment with funder goals and increased funding success rates**.

This section will explore:
- ✅ **How AI adapts to different industry grant writing needs**
- ✅ **Industry-specific funding sources and considerations**
- ✅ **The role of AI in customizing grant proposals for different sectors**
- ✅ **Practical AI prompts for industry-specific grant writing**

How AI Adapts to Different Industry Grant Writing Needs

AI-powered grant writing tools **adjust to different industries** by:

✈ **Understanding industry-specific language** – AI can tailor proposals using terminology relevant to each field.

✈ **Identifying sector-specific funding opportunities** – AI scans funding databases to match grants with industry needs.

✈ **Customizing evaluation metrics** – AI helps structure **impact measurements** based on industry expectations.

✈ **Ensuring compliance with sector regulations** – AI checks proposals for adherence to funding rules and reporting standards.

By using AI to **fine-tune proposals to each industry**, organizations can create **more relevant, compelling, and funder-aligned grant applications**.

Industry-Specific Funding Sources and Considerations

Different industries have distinct **funding sources and priorities**. Below is an overview of key industries and how AI can enhance grant writing in each.

1. Education (K-12 & Higher Education) 🎓

Key Funding Sources:
- ✅ Federal (U.S. Department of Education, NSF, Title I Grants)
- ✅ Foundations (Bill & Melinda Gates Foundation, Walton Family Foundation)
- ✅ State and Local Education Grants

How AI Helps:
- ◆ Identifies **STEM, literacy, and special education grants**
- ◆ Structures **data-driven impact statements**
- ◆ Generates **lesson plan-based grant proposals**

📌 **AI Prompt:** *"Find upcoming grants supporting STEM curriculum development in public high schools."*

---

2. Healthcare & Medical Research ⛨

Key Funding Sources:
- ✅ Government (NIH, CDC, HRSA)
- ✅ Private Foundations (Robert Wood Johnson Foundation, American Cancer Society)
- ✅ Hospitals and Research Institutions

How AI Helps:
- ◆ Drafts **research-based proposals** using clinical evidence
- ◆ Analyzes **healthcare policy trends** to align proposals with funder priorities
- ◆ Summarizes **scientific studies for literature reviews**

📌 **AI Prompt:** *"Summarize the latest research on rural healthcare disparities for a medical grant proposal."*

3. Nonprofits & Community Development 🤝

Key Funding Sources:
- ✅ Federal (HUD, USDA Community Grants)
- ✅ Private (United Way, Ford Foundation, Knight Foundation)
- ✅ Corporate Social Responsibility (CSR) Grants

How AI Helps:
- ♦ Creates **compelling community impact stories**
- ♦ Generates **quantitative and qualitative success metrics**
- ♦ Identifies **long-term sustainability funding**

✈ **AI Prompt:** *"Write an impact statement for a nonprofit grant supporting food security programs in urban communities."*

---

4. Environmental & Sustainability Grants 🌍

Key Funding Sources:
- ✅ Federal (EPA, Department of Energy)
- ✅ Philanthropic (The Nature Conservancy, Sierra Club Foundation)
- ✅ Private Sector (Green Business Innovation Grants)

How AI Helps:
- ♦ Crafts **climate impact assessments**
- ♦ Suggests **sustainable funding models**
- ♦ Structures **carbon reduction metrics for reporting**

✈ **AI Prompt:** *"Generate a grant proposal outline for a renewable energy research initiative."*

---

5. Technology & Innovation Startups 🚀

Key Funding Sources:
- ✅ Small Business Innovation Research (SBIR) & Small Business Technology Transfer (STTR) Grants
- ✅ Tech Venture Philanthropy
- ✅ Corporate Innovation Challenges

How AI Helps:
- Aligns proposals with **emerging tech trends**
- Creates **data visualizations for AI, robotics, or biotech funding**
- Suggests **commercialization strategies** for tech startups

📌 **AI Prompt:** *"Identify grants available for early-stage AI-driven healthcare startups."*

---

6. Arts, Culture, and Humanities 🎭

Key Funding Sources:
- National Endowment for the Arts (NEA)
- Private Arts Grants (Andrew W. Mellon Foundation, MacArthur Foundation)
- Local and Community-Based Cultural Grants

How AI Helps:
- Structures **creative grant proposals** with engaging narratives
- Suggests **arts impact measurement strategies**
- Generates **compelling artist statements and program descriptions**

📌 **AI Prompt:** *"Write a grant proposal for a public art installation promoting cultural heritage."*

How AI Customizes Grant Proposals for Each Industry

Grant Writing Element	How AI Customizes for Industry-Specific Needs
Problem Statement	AI uses **industry-specific statistics and trends** to justify funding needs.
Impact Measurement	AI aligns **outcome metrics** with funder expectations in healthcare, education, sustainability, etc.
Budget Justification	AI structures **cost estimates** based on industry norms.
Compliance and Regulations	AI ensures **adherence to sector-specific guidelines**, such as HIPAA for healthcare or Title I rules for education.

By tailoring **language, impact, and compliance considerations**, AI ensures proposals are **industry-optimized and funder-aligned**.

Case Study: AI-Driven Grant Writing Success in Higher Education

◆ **Background:** A university applied for a **$2 million STEM education grant** but needed to align the proposal with **funder priorities and student impact data**.

◆ **Challenges:**

- The original draft **lacked strong data on student learning outcomes**.
- The **budget needed clearer justifications** for faculty salaries and technology.
- The proposal required **better alignment with federal education priorities**.

◆ **How AI Helped:**

- **Impact Data Generation:** AI analyzed **national STEM achievement trends** to strengthen the proposal.
- **Budget Optimization:** AI structured **detailed cost justifications** for tech and faculty salaries.
- **Alignment with Federal Priorities:** AI **cross-referenced the proposal with NSF funding guidelines** to improve compliance.

◆ **Outcome:** The university **secured full grant funding**, expanding STEM programs for **2,500+ students**.

◆ **Key Takeaway:** AI-driven grant writing enhanced alignment, strengthened data presentation, and improved budget clarity.

Practical AI Prompts for Industry-Specific Grant Writing

1. Tailoring Problem Statements

★ *"Write a problem statement for an education grant focused on increasing STEM opportunities for underrepresented students."*

2. Customizing Impact Metrics

★ *"Generate measurable impact indicators for a community health outreach program."*

3. Ensuring Compliance with Sector Guidelines

📌 *"Review this proposal to ensure compliance with federal healthcare grant regulations."*

4. Adapting Budget Justifications to Industry Standards

📌 *"Write a budget justification for a university research grant covering faculty salaries and lab equipment."*

5. Finding Industry-Specific Grants

📌 *"Identify the top three grant funding sources for environmental sustainability initiatives in urban areas."*

By leveraging **AI-driven industry-specific strategies**, organizations can create **more compelling, targeted, and competitive grant proposals**.

Looking Ahead

Now that we've covered **how AI customizes grant writing for different industries**, the next section will focus on **case studies and success stories of AI-powered grant writing in action**—demonstrating real-world applications of AI in securing funding.

Reflection Questions:

1. How does your industry's grant writing process differ from others?
2. What AI tools could help you tailor grant proposals to industry-specific needs?
3. How can AI-driven impact measurement improve your grant success rates?

Chapter 3, Section 1 Summary

✓ AI adapts grant writing strategies to different industries, improving relevance and funder alignment.
✓ Each industry has unique funding sources, impact metrics, and compliance considerations.
✓ AI helps tailor problem statements, budget justifications, and outcome measurement to industry norms.
✓ Industry-specific AI prompts ensure proposals are competitive and well-structured.

Section 2: Case Studies and Success Stories of AI-Powered Grant Writing

AI-powered grant writing is not just theoretical—it has already transformed the way organizations **identify funding, draft proposals, and optimize applications**. By examining real-world examples, we can understand how AI has **enhanced efficiency, increased funding success rates, and improved proposal quality**.

This section will explore:
- ✅ **Real-world case studies of AI-powered grant writing success**
- ✅ **Lessons learned from organizations that leveraged AI for funding**
- ✅ **Key takeaways from AI-driven grant writing implementations**
- ✅ **Practical AI prompts for applying case study insights**

Case Study 1: AI-Optimized Grant Proposal Earns $3 Million for STEM Education Expansion

♦ **Background:** A public school district sought a **$3 million grant** to expand its **STEM curriculum and technology access**.

♦ **Challenges:**

- **Limited staff capacity** to write and refine the grant proposal.
- The proposal needed **data-driven justifications** for funding requests.
- **Alignment with federal education priorities** was unclear.

♦ **How AI Helped:**
✅ **Grant Matching:** AI identified a **Department of Education STEM Innovation Grant** that aligned with the district's needs.
✅ **Data-Driven Justifications:** AI integrated **national STEM education statistics** to strengthen the problem statement.
✅ **Budget Optimization:** AI generated **clear budget justifications** for lab equipment and teacher training.
✅ **Proposal Refinement:** AI-enhanced editing tools improved **clarity, engagement, and compliance**.

♦ **Outcome:**
🎉 The school district **won the $3 million grant**, enabling them to provide **1,500 students with new STEM resources**.

- **Key Takeaway:**
- AI-driven proposal refinement and budget justifications increase competitiveness and funding success rates.

Case Study 2: AI Streamlines Grant Process for Nonprofit Food Security Program

- **Background:** A nonprofit focused on **food insecurity** sought a **$250,000 community impact grant** but faced **time constraints** in the grant writing process.

- **Challenges:**

  - **Limited staff bandwidth** to research and draft the proposal.
  - The proposal required **personal impact stories** to strengthen funder appeal.
  - **Financial reporting and budget breakdowns** were difficult to structure.

- **How AI Helped:**
✅ **Automated Research:** AI-generated **state-level food insecurity statistics** to support the problem statement.
✅ **Storytelling Assistance:** AI structured **impact narratives** featuring community members who benefited from past programs.
✅ **Budget Formatting & Justifications:** AI organized **fund allocation reports** in funder-preferred formats.
✅ **Proposal Editing & Compliance Checks:** AI-assisted editing ensured **alignment with funder priorities**.

- **Outcome:**
🔎 The nonprofit secured the **$250,000 grant**, allowing them to expand food distribution services to **20% more families**.

- **Key Takeaway:**
- AI enhances research, storytelling, and financial justification, leading to well-structured, compelling proposals.

Case Study 3: AI-Driven Grant Strategy Boosts Healthcare Research Funding

♦ **Background:** A university research team applied for a **$5 million NIH grant** to study **rural healthcare access**.

♦ **Challenges:**

- Required a **highly technical grant proposal** with extensive literature review.
- Needed **compliance with NIH funding structure and reporting standards**.
- Faced **difficulty in refining key research objectives** for proposal clarity.

♦ **How AI Helped:**
✅ **Literature Review Automation:** AI summarized **recent peer-reviewed studies** on rural healthcare disparities.
✅ **Technical Proposal Writing Support:** AI structured the **methods and research design section** for clarity.
✅ **Regulatory Compliance Checks:** AI scanned the proposal for **alignment with NIH submission guidelines**.
✅ **Predictive Analysis for Funding Success:** AI compared past NIH-funded projects to identify **high-impact proposal themes**.

♦ **Outcome:**
🎉 The research team secured the **$5 million grant**, funding a **five-year study on rural healthcare solutions**.

♦ **Key Takeaway:**
♦ AI-powered research, compliance verification, and proposal refinement improve success in competitive funding pools.

Lessons Learned from AI-Driven Grant Writing Success

Across these case studies, common success factors emerged:

Lesson	Why It Matters	AI's Role
1. AI Increases Efficiency	AI reduces research and writing time, allowing teams to focus on strategic planning.	AI tools streamline **data gathering, proposal drafting, and budget structuring**.
2. Data-Driven Proposals Are More Competitive	Funders prefer applications that use strong evidence to support claims.	AI integrates **relevant statistics, trend analyses, and past funding data**.
3. AI Enhances Storytelling for Emotional Appeal	Impact stories make proposals more compelling.	AI structures **success stories and community testimonials**.
4. AI Optimizes Budget Justifications	Clearly justified expenses increase funder confidence.	AI formats **funding requests and financial narratives**.
5. AI Ensures Compliance and Alignment	Proposals that meet funder guidelines have higher approval rates.	AI scans for **compliance issues and suggests refinements**.

By leveraging AI strategically, organizations can **enhance proposal quality, improve funder alignment, and increase grant success rates**.

Practical AI Prompts for Applying Case Study Insights

1. Enhancing Data-Driven Justifications

📌 *"Find recent statistics on mental health access disparities to strengthen a healthcare grant proposal."*

2. Structuring a High-Impact Problem Statement

📌 *"Write a problem statement for a grant proposal addressing workforce shortages in STEM education."*

3. Automating Budget Formatting & Justification

📌 *"Generate a well-structured budget justification for a nonprofit expanding its literacy programs."*

4. Improving Narrative Storytelling

📌 *"Create a compelling success story for a grant proposal supporting first-generation college students."*

5. Ensuring Compliance with Funder Guidelines

📌 *"Check this grant proposal against [funder name]'s eligibility and formatting requirements."*

By using **AI-generated prompts and case study insights**, grant writers can **refine their proposals and improve funding success rates**.

Looking Ahead

Now that we've explored **real-world AI-driven grant writing success stories**, the next section will focus on **how to build an AI-powered grant writing workflow from start to finish**—providing a step-by-step guide to integrating AI into the grant development process.

Reflection Questions:

1. How can AI-driven insights improve your organization's grant writing success?
2. Which AI tools or strategies from these case studies could be applied to your funding efforts?
3. How can AI help refine your proposals for clarity, data integration, and funder alignment?

Chapter 3, Section 2 Summary

✅ **AI-powered grant writing has led to significant funding successes across industries.**
✅ **AI enhances efficiency, data-driven justifications, storytelling, and compliance.**
✅ **Lessons from real-world case studies highlight AI's impact on proposal quality.**
✅ **AI-generated prompts help apply best practices to future grant applications.**

Section 3: Building an AI-Powered Grant Writing Workflow from Start to Finish

A structured, **AI-enhanced grant writing workflow** helps organizations move efficiently from research to submission while ensuring high-quality, funder-aligned proposals. By integrating AI at each stage, grant writers can **streamline processes, improve proposal clarity, and increase funding success rates**.

This section will explore:
- ✅ **A step-by-step AI-powered grant writing workflow**
- ✅ **How AI enhances each stage of the process**
- ✅ **Tools and techniques for optimizing efficiency**
- ✅ **Practical AI prompts for each stage of grant writing**

Step-by-Step AI-Powered Grant Writing Workflow

An effective **AI-driven grant writing workflow** consists of six key stages:

Stage	Objective	How AI Helps
1. Research & Grant Identification	Find the best grant opportunities.	AI scans funding databases, matches grants to project needs, and summarizes eligibility criteria.
2. Planning & Structuring	Outline the proposal and gather key details.	AI generates structured templates and organizes proposal sections based on funder priorities.
3. Drafting Proposal Sections	Write a clear and compelling narrative.	AI generates problem statements, objectives, and impact statements with funder alignment.
4. Editing & Refining	Ensure clarity, readability, and compliance.	AI improves tone, grammar, and alignment with funding guidelines.
5. Budget Development & Justification	Create transparent, funder-friendly financial plans.	AI structures budget justifications and ensures financial compliance.
6. Final Review & Submission	Prepare a polished, funder-ready application.	AI checks formatting, verifies compliance, and generates submission checklists.

By following this **structured AI-driven workflow**, organizations can create **high-quality, data-driven, and funder-aligned proposals faster and more efficiently**.

Stage 1: Research & Grant Identification

- **Goal:** Find the best-fitting grant opportunities.
- **AI's Role:** Automates **funding searches, eligibility checks, and funder analysis**.

AI Tools & Strategies:

✓ **AI-Powered Grant Search Engines**: Grants.gov, Instrumentl, OpenGrants
✓ **Funder Alignment Analysis**: AI compares organizational goals with funder priorities.
✓ **Automated Grant Alerts**: AI tracks new opportunities and sends notifications.

📌 **AI Prompt:** *"Find education grants available for K-12 schools in STEM innovation with a deadline in the next 6 months."*

Stage 2: Planning & Structuring the Proposal

- **Goal:** Develop a clear proposal outline with strong alignment to funder goals.
- **AI's Role:** Generates **structured templates, organizes key sections, and suggests impactful headings**.

AI Tools & Strategies:

✓ **AI-Generated Proposal Outlines**: AI creates section headers and guiding questions.
✓ **Funder Requirement Mapping**: AI ensures all necessary components are included.
✓ **AI Brainstorming for Project Goals**: AI helps define objectives and expected outcomes.

📌 **AI Prompt:** *"Generate an outline for a grant proposal focusing on mental health services for underserved communities."*

Stage 3: Drafting Proposal Sections

- **Goal:** Write a compelling and funder-aligned grant proposal.
- **AI's Role:** Assists in drafting key sections with **data-driven insights and persuasive narratives**.

AI Tools & Strategies:

- ✓ **Problem Statement Generation**: AI integrates **statistics, research, and community needs**.
- ✓ **AI-Enhanced Impact Statements**: AI helps craft **emotionally compelling and funder-aligned narratives**.
- ✓ **SMART Objectives Development**: AI structures **Specific, Measurable, Achievable, Relevant, Time-bound** goals.

📌 **AI Prompt:** *"Write a problem statement for a grant proposal addressing rural healthcare disparities, incorporating current statistics."*

Stage 4: Editing & Refining the Proposal

- ♦ **Goal:** Improve clarity, coherence, and compliance before finalization.
- ♦ **AI's Role: Refines readability, grammar, and proposal tone** while ensuring compliance.

AI Tools & Strategies:

- ✓ **Grammar & Clarity Enhancement**: Grammarly, Hemingway Editor, ChatGPT
- ✓ **Compliance & Alignment Review**: AI cross-checks proposal language with funder priorities.
- ✓ **Readability & Tone Adjustments**: AI simplifies **complex sections** and enhances persuasiveness.

📌 **AI Prompt:** *"Improve the readability and engagement of this grant proposal while maintaining a professional tone."*

Stage 5: Budget Development & Justification

- ♦ **Goal:** Create a transparent, well-structured, and funder-compliant budget.
- ♦ **AI's Role:** Helps develop **clear financial breakdowns and justifications**.

AI Tools & Strategies:

- ✓ **Budget Justification Templates**: AI structures **detailed, funder-friendly justifications**.
- ✓ **Expense Breakdown Assistance**: AI calculates and aligns costs with project objectives.
- ✓ **Financial Compliance Checks**: AI ensures budgets meet **grant funding rules**.

📌 **AI Prompt:** *"Create a budget justification for a $250,000 grant covering salaries, equipment, and program costs."*

Stage 6: Final Review & Submission

- ♦ **Goal:** Ensure compliance, completeness, and error-free submission.
- ♦ **AI's Role:** Assists in **proofreading, compliance verification, and submission checklist generation**.

AI Tools & Strategies:

✓ **Final AI-Powered Proofreading**: Ensures **no grammatical or structural issues**.
✓ **Submission Checklist Generation**: AI creates a **step-by-step final review process**.
✓ **Grant Formatting & Compliance Checks**: AI ensures correct formatting, page limits, and eligibility alignment.

✈ **AI Prompt:** *"Generate a final checklist to ensure compliance with federal grant submission requirements."*

Case Study: AI-Powered Workflow Increases Grant Efficiency for a Nonprofit

- ♦ **Background:** A nonprofit applying for a **$500,000 federal community development grant** needed a **streamlined workflow**.

- ♦ **Challenges:**

  - Time-consuming research on funder alignment.
  - Manual drafting process delayed proposal submission.
  - Difficulties in structuring an effective budget justification.

- ♦ **How AI Helped:**

✓ **AI Grant Matching**: Identified **3 high-probability funding sources**.
✓ **Proposal Structuring & Drafting**: AI generated **a detailed proposal outline** with tailored sections.
✓ **Budget Justification Enhancement**: AI refined **expense descriptions** for clarity and compliance.

- ♦ **Outcome:**
🛠 The nonprofit **secured full funding**, completing the application **25% faster** than previous submissions.

♦ Key Takeaway:
♦ AI-driven workflows reduce manual workload, enhance proposal structure, and improve funding outcomes.

Practical AI Prompts for Building an AI-Powered Grant Workflow

1. Automating Grant Research

✦ *"Find upcoming grants for environmental sustainability projects with deadlines in the next six months."*

2. Structuring the Proposal Outline

✦ *"Generate a structured grant proposal outline for a technology education program for underserved youth."*

3. Drafting Key Proposal Sections

✦ *"Write a needs assessment for a grant proposal supporting affordable housing initiatives."*

4. Enhancing Clarity & Compliance

✦ *"Analyze this grant proposal and suggest refinements for better readability and alignment with funder priorities."*

5. Creating a Submission Checklist

✦ *"Generate a pre-submission checklist to ensure all grant application requirements are met."*

By following this **AI-powered workflow**, organizations can ensure **a smooth, efficient, and high-quality grant writing process from start to finish**.

What's Next?

Now that we've built an **AI-driven grant writing workflow**, the next section will explore **how to measure AI's impact on grant writing success and continuously refine AI strategies for better funding outcomes**.

Reflection Questions:

1. How can an AI-driven workflow enhance your organization's grant writing efficiency?
2. What AI tools could improve your research, drafting, or budgeting processes?
3. How can AI-generated insights help refine your proposal for better alignment and clarity?

Chapter 3, Section 3 Summary

✓ An AI-powered workflow streamlines research, drafting, editing, and submission.
✓ AI optimizes each stage, from grant matching to compliance verification.
✓ AI-generated prompts improve efficiency, clarity, and funder alignment.
✓ Integrating AI reduces manual workload and increases funding success rates.

Section 4: Measuring AI's Impact on Grant Writing Success

Implementing AI in grant writing is a strategic move, but **how do you measure its effectiveness?** Understanding the impact of AI tools on grant writing success helps organizations refine their approach, **improve efficiency, and maximize funding outcomes**.

This section will explore:
✓ **Key performance indicators (KPIs) for evaluating AI's effectiveness**
✓ **How AI-driven grant writing improves success rates**
✓ **Techniques for analyzing AI's impact on grant workflow and quality**
✓ **Practical AI prompts for assessing grant performance and optimization**

Key Performance Indicators (KPIs) for Evaluating AI's Effectiveness

To assess AI's impact on grant writing, organizations should track measurable KPIs, such as:

KPI	What It Measures	AI's Role
1. Grant Submission Rate	Number of grant applications submitted per cycle.	AI speeds up **research, drafting, and editing** to increase output.
2. Grant Approval Rate	Percentage of submitted proposals that secure funding.	AI improves **alignment with funder priorities and compliance checks**.
3. Proposal Drafting Time	Time required to complete a high-quality grant proposal.	AI automates **content structuring and section drafting**.
4. Editing and Compliance Efficiency	Time spent on refining proposals for clarity and alignment.	AI tools like **Grammarly and ChatGPT** enhance readability and compliance.
5. Budget Justification Clarity	Accuracy and transparency of budget narratives.	AI generates **detailed financial explanations** for funder confidence.

By tracking these KPIs, organizations can **quantify AI's effectiveness and make data-driven improvements**.

How AI-Driven Grant Writing Improves Success Rates

AI enhances grant writing **at multiple levels**, improving the likelihood of securing funding.

- **Better Grant Targeting**: AI analyzes funding trends and suggests the best-fit opportunities.
- **Stronger Data-Driven Proposals**: AI integrates **impact statistics and research-based justifications**.
- **Improved Readability & Clarity**: AI simplifies complex language and ensures professional tone.
- **Faster Submission Timelines**: AI reduces manual workload, allowing teams to submit more applications.
- **Enhanced Budget Justifications**: AI structures financial narratives that align with funder expectations.

📌 **AI Prompt:** *"Analyze our last five grant submissions and identify patterns in successful and unsuccessful applications."*

Techniques for Analyzing AI's Impact on Grant Workflow and Quality

To measure AI's effectiveness, organizations can **track, compare, and optimize** AI-assisted grant writing over time.

1. Comparative Analysis of AI-Enhanced vs. Non-AI Grant Proposals

✓ Compare approval rates, clarity scores, and submission speed between AI-assisted and manually written proposals.
📌 **AI Prompt:** *"Compare the readability and alignment of two grant proposals—one AI-assisted and one manually written."*

2. AI-Powered Grant Writing Time Efficiency Study

✓ Track how long each grant application stage takes **before and after** AI implementation.
📌 **AI Prompt:** *"Generate a timeline efficiency report showing how AI has reduced grant writing time by category (research, drafting, editing, etc.)."*

3. AI-Driven Proposal Quality Assessment

✓ Use AI to analyze **word choice, structure, and persuasive elements** across multiple proposals.
📌 **AI Prompt:** *"Evaluate this grant proposal's clarity, persuasiveness, and funder alignment using AI-driven analysis."*

4. Funder Feedback & AI Adjustments

✓ Collect funder feedback on grant proposals and refine AI-generated content accordingly.
📌 **AI Prompt:** *"Summarize funder feedback from the last three rejected grant proposals and suggest AI-driven improvements."*

Case Study: Measuring AI's Impact on a Nonprofit's Grant Success

◆ **Background:** A nonprofit dedicated to **youth mentorship programs** implemented AI to streamline its grant writing process.

◆ **Challenges:**

- **Limited staff resources** delayed proposal submissions.
- Proposals lacked **data-driven impact narratives**.
- Grant rejection feedback pointed to **unclear budget justifications**.

♠ **AI Implementation & Measurable Impact:**
✅ **Increased Grant Submission Rate**: From **3 to 7 applications per quarter**.
✅ **Higher Grant Approval Rate**: Approval rate improved from **20% to 45%** in one year.
✅ **Reduced Drafting Time**: Average proposal completion time decreased from **20 to 12 hours**.
✅ **Improved Budget Transparency**: Funders noted clearer **financial justifications**, boosting funder confidence.

♠ **Outcome:** The nonprofit **secured two new funding sources**, expanding its mentorship program by **30%**.

♠ **Key Takeaway:** Measuring AI-driven improvements in efficiency, clarity, and funder alignment leads to better funding success.

Practical AI Prompts for Assessing Grant Performance and Optimization

1. Evaluating Grant Submission Efficiency

✦ *"Analyze time efficiency in our last three AI-assisted grant applications and suggest improvements."*

2. Measuring Grant Approval Success Rates

✦ *"Generate a report comparing grant approval rates before and after integrating AI in our grant writing process."*

3. Improving Proposal Clarity and Readability

✦ *"Assess readability and funder alignment in our latest grant proposal and suggest AI-driven refinements."*

4. Enhancing Budget Transparency for Funders

✦ *"Analyze our budget justifications and recommend ways AI can improve clarity and transparency."*

5. Identifying Patterns in Rejected Grant Applications

📌 *"Review the feedback from declined grant applications and suggest AI-generated revisions to improve future success rates."*

By integrating **AI-driven analysis**, organizations can **refine their grant writing process and continuously enhance proposal quality for better funding outcomes**.

Looking Ahead

Now that we've covered **how to measure AI's impact on grant writing success**, the next section will focus on **best practices for continuous improvement in AI-enhanced grant writing**—ensuring organizations stay adaptive, innovative, and competitive in securing funding.

Reflection Questions:

1. What key performance indicators (KPIs) should you track to measure AI's effectiveness in grant writing?
2. How has AI improved efficiency and clarity in your grant proposals so far?
3. What further optimizations could AI bring to your grant development workflow?

Chapter 3, Section 4 Summary

✅ **Tracking KPIs helps organizations measure AI's impact on grant success.**
✅ **AI improves efficiency, clarity, data integration, and budget justifications.**
✅ **Comparing AI-enhanced vs. manual proposals reveals measurable improvements.**
✅ **Analyzing AI's effectiveness helps refine workflows and increase funding success.**

Section 5: Best Practices for Continuous Improvement in AI-Enhanced Grant Writing

AI in grant writing is not a one-time implementation—it requires **continuous refinement** to maximize efficiency and funding success. Organizations that consistently evaluate and improve their AI-powered grant writing strategies will stay ahead of **funding trends, proposal quality standards, and technological advancements**.

This section will explore:
✅ **Key best practices for continuous AI improvement**
✅ **How to refine AI-driven grant writing workflows over time**

✓ AI tools for ongoing learning and enhancement
✓ Practical AI prompts for optimizing grant writing strategies

Best Practices for Continuous AI-Enhanced Grant Writing Improvement

Best Practice	Why It Matters	How AI Helps
1. Regularly Evaluate AI-Generated Proposals	Ensures AI content aligns with evolving funder priorities.	AI tools review **proposal effectiveness and alignment** with past successful grants.
2. Incorporate Human Expertise & Creativity	AI generates drafts, but human insight refines and enhances them.	AI suggests **edits and improvements**, but humans **add personalization and strategy**.
3. Update AI Training Data with Latest Grant Trends	Keeps AI-informed recommendations relevant and up to date.	AI analyzes **recently funded projects and emerging grant requirements**.
4. Track AI-Driven Grant Writing Metrics	Helps measure success rates and identify areas for improvement.	AI generates **performance analytics** on submission efficiency and approval rates.
5. Seek Funders' Feedback and Implement AI Adjustments	Understanding funder preferences improves future applications.	AI synthesizes **feedback themes** from funders and suggests refinements.

By continuously **evaluating, refining, and adapting** AI strategies, organizations can **enhance their grant writing process and increase their funding success rate**.

How to Refine AI-Driven Grant Writing Workflows Over Time

1. Conduct Regular AI Performance Reviews

✓ Analyze which AI-generated grant proposals performed best and why.

📌 **AI Prompt:** *"Compare the readability and approval rates of our last five AI-assisted grant proposals."*

2. Update AI Tools with New Industry Data

✓ Train AI models with the **latest funding trends, policy changes, and sector priorities**.
✦ **AI Prompt:** *"Summarize recent trends in federal grant funding for healthcare innovation."*

---

3. Customize AI Outputs Based on Funder Preferences

✓ Adjust AI prompts to reflect **specific language, priorities, and impact metrics** preferred by funders.
✦ **AI Prompt:** *"Rewrite this grant proposal's problem statement to align with [specific funder's] priorities."*

---

4. Balance AI Automation with Human-Led Creativity

✓ AI streamlines technical tasks, but human experts ensure **authenticity, emotion, and persuasive storytelling**.
✦ **AI Prompt:** *"Enhance the emotional appeal and storytelling in this grant proposal impact statement."*

---

5. Implement AI-Driven Proposal A/B Testing

✓ Submit different AI-enhanced grant proposal versions to assess **which styles and structures lead to higher funding success**.
✦ **AI Prompt:** *"Generate two variations of an executive summary for a STEM education grant proposal."*

By consistently **analyzing AI-generated content, integrating feedback, and updating strategies**, grant writers can **continuously improve the effectiveness of AI-powered proposals**.

AI Tools for Ongoing Learning and Enhancement

To keep **AI-assisted grant writing efficient and high-performing**, organizations can use the following tools for **learning, refining, and adapting**:

AI Tool	Function	Best For
Grants.gov & Instrumentl	Tracks **funding trends and grant opportunities**.	Ensuring AI recommendations align with **latest funding priorities**.
ChatGPT & Gemini AI	Generates **multiple proposal versions** for testing and refinement.	Enhancing **writing quality and strategic alignment**.
Hemingway Editor & Grammarly	Evaluates **clarity, tone, and readability** of AI-generated text.	Improving **proposal engagement and professional tone**.
Tableau & Power BI	Analyzes **grant performance metrics and success trends**.	Measuring **AI's impact on submission and approval rates**.
Notion AI & Trello AI	Organizes grant writing workflows and team collaboration.	Ensuring **efficient AI-driven workflow management**.

By **leveraging these tools strategically**, organizations can refine AI usage and **adapt to evolving grant writing needs**.

Case Study: How Continuous AI Refinement Improved Grant Success

♦ **Background:** A nonprofit specializing in **early childhood education** initially struggled with grant application success despite using AI-generated proposals.

♦ **Challenges:**

- AI-generated proposals lacked emotional engagement and storytelling.
- Funders provided feedback that proposals needed more human impact stories.
- The grant writing team had trouble customizing AI outputs for different funders.

♦ **How AI Refinement Helped:**
✓ **Added More Human Personalization:** AI-generated content was edited to incorporate **real-life impact narratives**.
✓ **Tracked Proposal Success Metrics:** AI-generated reports revealed that **data-backed proposals had higher success rates**.
✓ **Customized AI Outputs for Funders:** AI-generated text was refined to **match the preferred language and priorities of different funders**.

♦ **Outcome:**
🎉 The nonprofit **increased its grant approval rate by 50%** within one year by continuously refining AI-assisted proposals based on **funder feedback and success patterns**.

♦ **Key Takeaway:** AI is most effective when continuously refined, personalized, and strategically implemented.

Practical AI Prompts for Optimizing Grant Writing Strategies

1. Improving AI Proposal Quality Based on Past Success

📌 *"Analyze past successful grant applications and suggest ways to improve our next proposal."*

2. Enhancing AI-Generated Impact Statements

📌 *"Rewrite this impact statement to include a stronger emotional connection with the audience."*

3. Customizing Proposals for Different Funders

📌 *"Modify this proposal's tone and language to align with [specific funder's] guidelines and priorities."*

4. Tracking Grant Performance Metrics

📌 *"Generate a success rate comparison of AI-assisted vs. non-AI grant applications over the last two years."*

5. Refining Budget Justifications with AI

📌 *"Analyze our last three budget justifications and suggest improvements in clarity and alignment with funder expectations."*

By using AI-driven insights to **continuously optimize grant writing strategies**, organizations can **enhance efficiency, increase approval rates, and stay ahead in the funding landscape**.

Looking Ahead

Now that we've covered **best practices for continuous improvement in AI-enhanced grant writing**, the next chapter will focus on **common challenges and solutions when implementing AI in grant writing**—helping organizations overcome obstacles and maximize AI's potential.

Reflection Questions:

1. How often does your organization review and refine AI-assisted grant writing strategies?
2. What key improvements have you noticed in AI-generated proposals, and where could further optimization help?
3. How can AI be balanced with human expertise to create stronger, funder-aligned grant proposals?

Chapter 3, Section 5 Summary

✅ **Continuous improvement is key to maximizing AI's impact on grant writing success.**
✅ **Tracking proposal effectiveness and refining AI-generated content leads to higher funding success rates.**
✅ **Customizing AI outputs based on funder feedback enhances proposal alignment.**
✅ **Balancing AI automation with human insight results in stronger, more compelling proposals.**

Chapter 4: Overcoming Challenges and Pitfalls in AI-Driven Grant Writing

Section 1: Common Challenges When Using AI for Grant Writing

While AI has revolutionized grant writing by improving efficiency and proposal quality, it is not without its **challenges**. Understanding the common pitfalls of AI-driven grant writing helps organizations **avoid mistakes, optimize workflows, and ensure AI enhances—rather than hinders—their funding success**.

This section will explore:
- The most common challenges in AI-powered grant writing
- How to recognize and address AI-related pitfalls
- The role of human oversight in AI-generated content
- Practical AI prompts for troubleshooting grant writing issues

Common Challenges in AI-Driven Grant Writing

Challenge	Why It's a Problem	How to Overcome It
1. Over-Reliance on AI Without Human Input	AI-generated proposals may lack **depth, personalization, and emotional appeal**.	**Review AI-generated drafts manually** and add **authentic storytelling and insights**.
2. Generic or Repetitive AI-Generated Content	AI may produce **formulaic or repetitive language**, making proposals **less compelling**.	Use **AI customization prompts** to refine wording and ensure funder-specific language.
3. Compliance & Formatting Issues	AI doesn't always adhere to **strict funder guidelines** on formatting, word limits, or structure.	Manually review **submission requirements** and adjust AI-generated content accordingly.
4. Ethical Concerns & Data Privacy	AI tools may **store or expose sensitive grant information**.	Use **secure AI platforms** and avoid **inputting confidential data**.
5. Difficulty in Aligning AI Content with Funders' Priorities	AI may **miss the nuances** of specific grant eligibility and impact expectations.	Train AI by **feeding it past successful proposals** and funder guidelines.

By recognizing these **challenges early**, organizations can **leverage AI effectively while maintaining high-quality, funder-aligned proposals**.

The Role of Human Oversight in AI-Generated Grant Writing

AI should be viewed as an **assistant, not a replacement** for human expertise. Human oversight ensures:

- **Authenticity & Emotional Connection** – Funders value personal stories and mission-driven narratives.
- **Compliance & Grant-Specific Customization** – AI may overlook specific **funder preferences or eligibility criteria**.
- **Strategic Adaptation to Funders' Priorities** – AI-generated content must be refined to align with **unique funder expectations**.
- **Final Decision-Making & Proposal Structuring** – Humans must ensure that AI-enhanced proposals are **logically structured, impactful, and well-supported**.

✦ **AI Prompt:** *"Refine this AI-generated grant proposal to improve emotional engagement and storytelling."*

How to Recognize and Address AI-Related Pitfalls

1. Avoiding AI-Generated Repetition & Generic Content

- AI may reuse phrases or **lack originality in proposal writing**.
- **Solution:** Use AI prompts to generate **multiple variations** of key sections.
- **AI Prompt:** *"Provide three different ways to phrase this project objective to avoid repetition."*

2. Ensuring Grant Compliance & Formatting Accuracy

- AI-generated content **may not follow exact funder formatting rules**.
- **Solution:** Manually check word limits, budget requirements, and formatting before submission.
- **AI Prompt:** *"Check this proposal for alignment with [specific funder's] formatting and submission requirements."*

3. Preventing Data Privacy Risks in AI-Powered Grant Writing

- AI tools may store inputted text, creating **security concerns for proprietary grant strategies**.
- **Solution:** Use **secure AI tools** and avoid inputting **confidential funding details**.
- **AI Prompt:** *"Suggest security best practices for using AI in grant writing without compromising data privacy."*

4. Improving AI Alignment with Funder Priorities

- AI-generated content **may not emphasize the specific mission and funding goals of a grant opportunity**.
- **Solution:** Customize AI outputs using funder guidelines and **past successful proposals**.
- **AI Prompt:** *"Rewrite this executive summary to better align with [specific funder's] priorities and mission."*

Case Study: Overcoming AI Limitations in Grant Writing

- **Background:** A nonprofit focused on **mental health awareness** adopted AI-powered grant writing but initially struggled with **proposal effectiveness and funder alignment**.

- **Challenges:**

  - AI-generated content **lacked emotional depth and storytelling**.
  - **Formatting and compliance errors** resulted in rejected applications.
  - The AI **failed to align with unique funder priorities**, making proposals **less competitive**.

- **How the Organization Addressed These Issues:**

✅ **Added Human Review for Emotional Appeal** – AI-generated drafts were refined to include **real-life impact stories**.
✅ **Manually Verified Formatting & Compliance** – Grant teams checked word limits and adjusted structure before submission.
✅ **Customized AI Prompts for Funder-Specific Content** – AI was trained with **past successful grant language** to improve alignment.

- **Outcome:**

🎉 The organization's **grant success rate increased by 40%**, and proposals became **more competitive and compelling**.

- **Key Takeaway:** AI is a powerful tool but requires human oversight for personalization, compliance, and strategic funder alignment.

Practical AI Prompts for Troubleshooting Grant Writing Issues

1. Identifying and Fixing Repetitive AI-Generated Content

📌 *"Rewrite this project description to remove redundant phrasing while maintaining clarity."*

2. Ensuring Compliance with Funder Guidelines

📌 *"Check this grant proposal against [specific funder] requirements and suggest necessary modifications."*

3. Enhancing Emotional Impact in AI-Generated Text

📌 *"Make this impact statement more compelling by adding personal stories and emotional appeal."*

4. Securing Confidential Information in AI-Generated Proposals

📌 *"What are best practices for using AI in grant writing while maintaining data privacy and security?"*

5. Improving AI Alignment with Funder Priorities

📌 *"Adjust this grant proposal to better match the goals of [specific funder]."*

By proactively **addressing AI challenges and applying targeted solutions**, organizations can **maximize AI's potential while ensuring high-quality, funder-aligned proposals.**

Looking Ahead

Now that we've identified **common challenges and solutions in AI-powered grant writing**, the next section will focus on **navigating ethical considerations and responsible AI use in funding applications**—ensuring organizations adopt AI **transparently, ethically, and effectively.**

Reflection Questions:

1. How can your organization balance AI automation with human expertise in grant writing?
2. What are the most common AI-related challenges you've encountered, and how can they be addressed?
3. How can you refine AI-generated proposals to better align with funder expectations and requirements?

Chapter 4, Section 1 Summary

✅ **AI-powered grant writing presents challenges such as repetition, lack of emotional depth, and compliance issues.**

✅ **Human oversight is critical to ensuring AI-generated proposals are funder-aligned, engaging, and compliant.**

✅ **Using AI strategically**—while avoiding security risks and funder misalignment—**improves funding success rates.**

✅ **AI prompts and workflow adjustments help organizations refine AI-driven grant writing for maximum effectiveness.**

Section 2: Navigating Ethical Considerations and Responsible AI Use in Grant Writing

As AI becomes more integrated into grant writing, organizations must address **ethical considerations** to ensure AI is used responsibly. Transparency, data security, and **maintaining the human element** are crucial to ethical AI implementation in funding applications.

This section will explore:
- ✓ **Key ethical concerns when using AI in grant writing**
- ✓ **Best practices for responsible AI adoption**
- ✓ **How to balance AI efficiency with human judgment**
- ✓ **Practical AI prompts for ensuring ethical grant writing**

Key Ethical Considerations in AI-Powered Grant Writing

Ethical Concern	Why It Matters	Best Practices
1. Transparency in AI-Generated Content	Funders value **authenticity and originality** in proposals.	Clearly state when AI assists in drafting proposals and ensure **human review before submission**.
2. Data Privacy & Security	AI tools may store **sensitive financial and organizational information**.	Use **secure AI platforms**, avoid **inputting confidential data**, and follow funder privacy regulations.
3. Avoiding AI-Generated Bias	AI may reflect **biases in training data**, leading to inequitable language or recommendations.	Manually review AI-generated text for **inclusivity and neutrality**.
4. Maintaining Human-Led Decision Making	AI should support, not replace, **strategic judgment and storytelling**.	Use AI for **efficiency**, but ensure humans **craft the final proposal narrative**.
5. Avoiding Plagiarism & AI-Generated Copyright Issues	AI-generated text may **accidentally replicate existing content**.	Check AI-written proposals for **originality and proper citation of research or data**.

By following these ethical best practices, organizations can **maximize AI's benefits while ensuring grant proposals remain authentic, secure, and fair**.

Best Practices for Responsible AI Use in Grant Writing

1. Disclosing AI Assistance in Proposal Writing

✓ Funders may appreciate knowing how AI was used in grant development.
📌 **Best Practice:** Use a disclosure statement:
"This proposal was developed with AI-assisted tools to enhance clarity and efficiency, with final content reviewed and refined by our grant writing team."

📌 **AI Prompt:** *"Generate a professional AI disclosure statement for a grant proposal submission."*

---

2. Protecting Sensitive Grant Data

✓ AI platforms may store or process user-generated content, raising **data privacy concerns**.
📌 **Best Practice:** Use **local AI models** or encrypted cloud-based platforms for AI-assisted writing.

📌 **AI Prompt:** *"List best practices for securing grant-related data when using AI writing tools."*

---

3. Addressing Bias in AI-Generated Proposals

✓ AI may **reinforce stereotypes** or overlook diverse perspectives in grant writing.
📌 **Best Practice:** Manually review AI-generated text for **inclusivity and unbiased language**.

📌 **AI Prompt:** *"Analyze this grant proposal for potential biases and suggest inclusive language improvements."*

---

4. Ensuring Ethical Storytelling in AI-Assisted Proposals

✓ AI should support **ethical, consent-based storytelling** when incorporating impact stories.
📌 **Best Practice:** Always obtain **permission for personal testimonials** and review AI-enhanced narratives for accuracy.

📌 **AI Prompt:** *"Ensure this impact statement maintains ethical storytelling and respects participant confidentiality."*

5. Conducting AI-Assisted Plagiarism and Originality Checks

✓ AI-generated text may unintentionally **mimic existing content**, raising plagiarism risks.
📌 **Best Practice:** Use plagiarism detection tools (Grammarly, Turnitin, or Copyscape) to verify originality before submission.

📌 **AI Prompt:** *"Check this AI-generated grant proposal for originality and citation accuracy."*

How to Balance AI Efficiency with Human Judgment

AI should **enhance**, not replace, human expertise in grant writing. The **ideal balance** ensures AI **handles repetitive tasks**, while humans **bring strategic thinking and emotional intelligence** to proposals.

Task	Best Done by AI	Best Done by Humans
Research & Data Summarization	AI can scan funding databases and summarize reports.	Humans verify **accuracy and relevance** of the data.
Proposal Drafting & Structuring	AI generates structured outlines and drafts key sections.	Humans refine **language, tone, and storytelling**.
Editing & Compliance Checking	AI proofreads for grammar and formatting errors.	Humans check for **alignment with funder priorities**.
Budget Justifications & Financial Narratives	AI organizes numbers and structures justifications.	Humans ensure **financial accuracy and funder expectations** are met.

By maintaining **human-led decision-making**, organizations can ensure AI **boosts productivity without compromising quality or ethical standards**.

📌 **AI Prompt:** *"Analyze this grant proposal draft and suggest which sections should be reviewed for human refinement."*

Case Study: Ethical AI Use in Nonprofit Grant Writing

♦ **Background:** A nonprofit organization used AI to streamline its **grant proposal development for mental health services** but faced ethical challenges in storytelling and compliance.

- **Challenges:**

  - AI-generated **impact statements included fictitious or exaggerated details**, which funders found misleading.
  - AI-written sections contained **unintentional biases**, such as **assuming certain demographic needs** without factual backing.
  - The team struggled with **data privacy concerns** when inputting financial projections into AI tools.

- **How the Organization Addressed These Issues:**

  ✓ **Revised AI-Generated Narratives for Accuracy** – The team ensured **all testimonials were real and properly cited**.

  ✓ **Implemented Bias-Checking Procedures** – AI-generated text was **reviewed for neutrality and inclusivity** before submission.

  ✓ **Used Encrypted AI Tools for Sensitive Data** – Financial projections were **processed securely** without exposing confidential information.

- **Outcome:**

  The nonprofit improved its **funder credibility and compliance rates**, leading to a **30% increase in successful grant awards**.

- **Key Takeaway:** AI must be used transparently and ethically to ensure accuracy, inclusivity, and responsible storytelling in grant writing.

Practical AI Prompts for Ensuring Ethical Grant Writing

1. Reviewing AI-Generated Proposals for Accuracy

★ *"Check this grant proposal for accuracy and factual integrity in all sections."*

2. Ensuring Inclusivity & Bias-Free Language

★ *"Analyze this proposal for biased language and suggest more inclusive alternatives."*

3. Creating an AI Transparency Disclosure for Funders

★ *"Draft a brief AI disclosure statement explaining how AI was used in this grant proposal."*

4. Strengthening Ethical Impact Statements

📌 *"Ensure this impact story is ethically written and maintains factual accuracy without embellishment."*

5. Implementing AI Security Best Practices in Grant Writing

📌 *"List steps to secure sensitive financial data when using AI for grant proposals."*

By following these best practices, organizations can **harness AI's benefits responsibly while maintaining trust, transparency, and funder confidence.**

Looking Ahead

Now that we've explored **ethical AI considerations in grant writing**, the next section will focus on **troubleshooting AI-generated grant proposals**—helping organizations refine AI-enhanced content for **clarity, compliance, and effectiveness**.

Reflection Questions:

1. How can your organization implement AI responsibly in grant writing while maintaining transparency?
2. What steps can you take to ensure AI-generated proposals are inclusive and unbiased?
3. How can AI enhance efficiency without compromising ethical storytelling and data privacy?

Chapter 4, Section 2 Summary

✅ Ethical AI use in grant writing requires transparency, security, and human oversight.
✅ Avoiding bias, ensuring factual accuracy, and protecting data are critical for responsible AI adoption.
✅ Balancing AI efficiency with human-led refinement leads to better funder-aligned proposals.
✅ By following best practices, organizations can maintain credibility, compliance, and ethical storytelling.

Section 3: Troubleshooting AI-Generated Grant Proposals for Clarity, Compliance, and Effectiveness

While AI significantly enhances grant writing efficiency, **AI-generated proposals can still contain errors, inconsistencies, or compliance gaps**. Organizations must carefully **troubleshoot and refine** AI-generated content to ensure that proposals are clear, compelling, and aligned with funder requirements.

This section will explore:
- ✅ Common issues in AI-generated grant proposals
- ✅ Techniques for improving clarity, compliance, and persuasiveness
- ✅ How to fine-tune AI prompts for better proposal outputs
- ✅ Practical AI prompts for troubleshooting grant writing issues

Common Issues in AI-Generated Grant Proposals

Issue	Why It's a Problem	How to Fix It
1. Overuse of Generic or Repetitive Language	AI-generated content may sound **formulaic and redundant**, reducing engagement.	Refine AI prompts to encourage **varied, dynamic phrasing** and **funding-specific language**.
2. Lack of Emotional Appeal & Storytelling	AI may create **factual but dry narratives** lacking human connection.	Incorporate **personal stories, real-world impact, and mission-driven language**.
3. Non-Compliance with Grant Guidelines	AI-generated text may exceed **word limits** or lack required sections.	Manually check **formatting, section requirements, and eligibility criteria** before submission.
4. Weak Problem Statements	AI may generate **broad, unfocused problem descriptions** that lack data-backed justification.	Strengthen problem statements with **quantitative research, statistics, and urgency**.
5. Misaligned Budget Justifications	AI-generated budgets may lack **detailed financial rationale**, leading to funder skepticism.	Use AI to format **transparent cost breakdowns**, but ensure **manual review for accuracy**.

By systematically **troubleshooting AI-generated proposals**, organizations can **enhance clarity, compliance, and persuasiveness**.

Techniques for Improving Clarity, Compliance, and Effectiveness

1. Eliminating Generic & Repetitive Language

✅ AI-generated text sometimes **repeats phrases or lacks variety**.
📌 **Solution:** Use AI to generate **multiple phrasing variations** for key proposal sections.

📌 **AI Prompt:** *"Rewrite this section to remove redundancy and enhance engagement with varied language."*

2. Strengthening Emotional Appeal & Storytelling

✅ AI-generated content often lacks **human emotion and compelling impact stories**.
📌 **Solution:** Blend **AI-assisted writing with human-authored impact statements**.

📌 **AI Prompt:** *"Revise this impact statement to make it more emotionally compelling and funder-oriented."*

3. Ensuring Grant Compliance & Formatting Accuracy

✅ AI-generated proposals **may not follow exact submission guidelines**.
📌 **Solution:** Review funder requirements **before finalizing AI-generated text**.

📌 **AI Prompt:** *"Check this proposal against [specific funder's] submission guidelines for formatting and compliance errors."*

4. Refining Problem Statements with Data-Driven Justifications

✅ AI may generate **broad or weak problem statements** that lack urgency.
📌 **Solution:** Integrate **quantitative research, statistics, and funder-aligned priorities**.

📌 **AI Prompt:** *"Enhance this problem statement with relevant data and statistics to justify funding needs."*

5. Improving Budget Justifications for Funders

✓ AI-generated budgets sometimes **lack strong cost explanations**.
📌 **Solution:** Ensure justifications **clearly connect budget items to program goals**.

📌 **AI Prompt:** *"Rewrite this budget justification to clearly explain the necessity of each expense."*

How to Fine-Tune AI Prompts for Better Proposal Outputs

AI-generated grant proposals are **only as good as the prompts used to create them**. By **refining AI prompts**, organizations can ensure proposals are **stronger, more persuasive, and more funder-aligned**.

AI Prompt Issue	Common Problem	How to Improve It
Vague Prompting	Results in **generalized, low-impact AI-generated content**.	Use **specific funder goals, sector language, and proposal structure** in prompts.
Lack of Tone Customization	AI content may sound **too formal or too casual**.	Specify **desired tone (persuasive, engaging, professional)** in AI prompts.
Not Providing Enough Context	AI may generate **misaligned content** if funder priorities aren't included.	Provide **funder mission statements, past successful grants, or target audience** in prompts.

Example: Weak vs. Strong AI Prompts for Grant Writing

⊘ **Weak AI Prompt:**
"Write a grant proposal for a literacy program."

✅ **Strong AI Prompt:**
"Write a grant proposal for a literacy program serving low-income elementary students in urban communities. The proposal should include a problem statement with relevant statistics, measurable objectives, a detailed budget justification, and alignment with the priorities of the [specific funder]."

By **customizing AI prompts effectively**, organizations can generate **higher-quality, funder-aligned grant proposals**.

Case Study: Troubleshooting AI-Generated Grant Proposals for a Nonprofit

♦ **Background:** A nonprofit applying for a **$500,000 workforce development grant** used AI to generate proposal drafts but faced **quality and compliance challenges**.

♦ **Challenges:**

- The **problem statement lacked data-driven justifications**.
- The **budget justification was vague**, making costs appear arbitrary.
- The proposal **did not follow the funder's specific formatting guidelines**.

♦ **How the Nonprofit Fixed These Issues:**
✓ **Refined AI Prompts to Strengthen Problem Statements** – AI-generated text was enhanced with **current workforce data** and **regional employment statistics**.
✓ **Manually Adjusted Budget Justifications** – AI-assisted cost breakdowns were revised for **clearer alignment with project goals**.
✓ **Formatted Proposal for Compliance** – The proposal was manually checked against the funder's **required structure, font size, and page limits**.

♦ **Outcome:**
🎉 The nonprofit **successfully secured the $500,000 grant** by improving AI-generated text through **strategic troubleshooting and human oversight**.

♦ **Key Takeaway:** AI speeds up grant writing, but final refinement, compliance checks, and funder-specific customization remain essential.

Practical AI Prompts for Troubleshooting Grant Writing Issues

1. Fixing Repetitive or Generic Language in AI-Generated Text

★ *"Rewrite this section to remove redundancy and make the language more engaging and persuasive."*

2. Strengthening Impact Statements with Emotional Appeal

★ *"Enhance this impact statement with a compelling personal story and strong emotional appeal."*

3. Ensuring Compliance with Funder Guidelines

📌 *"Check this proposal against [specific funder's] submission requirements and highlight any compliance issues."*

4. Refining Budget Justifications for Clarity and Transparency

📌 *"Improve this budget justification by clearly linking each expense to the project's outcomes and funder expectations."*

5. Improving Problem Statements with Data and Urgency

📌 *"Strengthen this problem statement by adding recent statistics and explaining the urgency of addressing this issue."*

By using these **AI prompts and troubleshooting techniques**, organizations can **refine AI-generated proposals to maximize clarity, compliance, and effectiveness**.

Looking Ahead

Now that we've covered **how to troubleshoot AI-generated grant proposals**, the next section will focus on **real-world success stories and lessons learned from AI-powered grant writing implementations**—helping organizations apply best practices for funding success.

Reflection Questions:

1. What are the most common AI-generated errors you've encountered in grant proposals, and how did you fix them?
2. How can you refine your AI prompts to generate stronger, more funder-aligned proposals?
3. What troubleshooting techniques will you implement to enhance the effectiveness of AI-powered grant writing?

Chapter 4, Section 3 Summary

✅ AI-generated proposals often require troubleshooting to improve clarity, compliance, and persuasiveness.
✅ Common issues include repetitive language, weak problem statements, and misaligned budget justifications.
✅ Fine-tuning AI prompts ensures stronger, more relevant grant proposals.
✅ Human oversight remains essential for refining AI-assisted grant writing for funding success.

Section 4: Real-World Success Stories and Lessons Learned from AI-Powered Grant Writing

AI-powered grant writing is already transforming the funding landscape for **nonprofits, educational institutions, healthcare organizations, and businesses**. By examining **real-world success stories**, we can identify **key lessons and best practices** that organizations can apply to maximize their funding potential.

This section will explore:
- ✅ **Real-world examples of AI-enhanced grant writing success**
- ✅ **Lessons learned from organizations that effectively implemented AI**
- ✅ **How AI helped overcome specific grant-writing challenges**
- ✅ **Practical AI prompts for applying lessons learned to future grant proposals**

Case Study 1: AI Helps Nonprofit Secure $1.2 Million in Housing Grants

♦ **Background:** A nonprofit focused on **affordable housing** applied for multiple federal and private grants but struggled with proposal consistency and funder alignment.

♦ **Challenges:**

- The team spent **too much time** manually writing and revising grant applications.
- Proposals **lacked a standardized structure**, making it difficult to maintain quality.
- Funders wanted **data-driven justifications**, but the organization struggled to integrate relevant statistics.

♦ **How AI Helped:**
✅ **Automated Grant Research:** AI identified **six high-potential grants** aligned with the nonprofit's mission.
✅ **Structured Proposal Templates:** AI generated **consistent proposal outlines** tailored to each funder's requirements.
✅ **Data Integration:** AI extracted **relevant housing crisis statistics** to strengthen problem statements.

♦ **Outcome:**
🎉 The nonprofit **won three grants totaling $1.2 million**, allowing them to expand their affordable housing program to **300+ families**.

- **Key Takeaway:**
- AI improves efficiency, proposal standardization, and data-driven storytelling, leading to higher grant success rates.

AI Prompt: *"Find relevant statistics on urban housing shortages to strengthen a grant proposal for affordable housing funding."*

Case Study 2: AI Speeds Up Grant Writing for STEM Education Initiative

- **Background:** A school district sought funding for a **$500,000 STEM education program** but faced **staffing limitations** that made it difficult to draft multiple grant proposals.

- **Challenges:**

  - Teachers had **limited time** to dedicate to grant writing.
  - The district needed **multiple applications submitted simultaneously**.
  - Funders required **customized proposals** aligned with specific STEM education goals.

- **How AI Helped:**
- **Proposal Generation:** AI drafted **five tailored grant proposals** in a fraction of the time.
- **Editing & Compliance Checks:** AI ensured **each proposal met funder guidelines**.
- **Impact Storytelling:** AI helped **craft student success stories** to illustrate program effectiveness.

- **Outcome:**
- The district **won funding for three grants** and launched STEM programs in **10 additional schools**.

- **Key Takeaway:**
- AI enables organizations to scale grant writing efforts and submit more high-quality proposals with fewer resources.

AI Prompt: *"Generate a grant proposal outline for a STEM education program targeting underrepresented students."*

Case Study 3: AI Improves Budget Justifications for Healthcare Research Grant

♦ **Background:** A university research team applied for a **$2 million NIH grant** to study **healthcare disparities in rural communities** but faced challenges with **budget justification clarity**.

♦ **Challenges:**

- Past proposals had **funding rejections due to unclear cost justifications**.
- Budget sections were **overly complex** and difficult for reviewers to follow.
- The team needed **compliance with NIH financial reporting standards**.

♦ **How AI Helped:**
✓ **Refined Budget Justifications:** AI created **clear, structured explanations** for each budget line item.
✓ **Simplified Financial Reporting:** AI formatted **data tables and expense breakdowns** to align with NIH guidelines.
✓ **Compliance Check:** AI ensured **funding requests adhered to NIH regulations**.

♦ **Outcome:**
🎉 The university secured the **$2 million grant**, funding a **five-year healthcare study** impacting **rural patient access to care**.

♦ **Key Takeaway:**
♦ AI enhances budget clarity and compliance, increasing funder confidence in financial management.

✈ **AI Prompt:** *"Improve the clarity of this budget justification by making each expense directly connect to project outcomes."*

Lessons Learned from AI-Powered Grant Writing Success

Across these case studies, several **common lessons emerged**:

Lesson	Why It Matters	How AI Supports This
1. AI Saves Time Without Sacrificing Quality	AI enables teams to write and submit **more proposals in less time**.	AI automates **drafting, editing, and formatting**, improving efficiency.
2. Data-Driven Proposals Have Higher Success Rates	Funders prefer proposals that are **backed by statistics and research**.	AI extracts **relevant data** to strengthen problem statements and justifications.
3. AI Ensures Consistency Across Multiple Proposals	Standardized proposals maintain **clarity and professionalism**.	AI generates **structured templates** for uniformity.
4. Budget Transparency Boosts Funder Confidence	Clear, detailed budgets **increase grant approval rates**.	AI structures **well-explained budget justifications**.
5. AI Enables More Personalized, Funder-Aligned Proposals	Tailored proposals **match funder goals, increasing competitiveness**.	AI customizes proposals based on **funder mission statements**.

By applying these **lessons learned**, organizations can **use AI more effectively to improve grant writing success rates**.

Practical AI Prompts for Applying Lessons to Future Grant Writing

1. Scaling Grant Writing Without Overburdening Staff

📌 *"Generate a structured grant proposal draft for a workforce development program, ensuring alignment with funder priorities."*

2. Strengthening Data-Backed Justifications

📌 *"Find recent statistics on mental health disparities to support a community health grant proposal."*

3. Creating Funder-Specific Proposal Templates

✦ *"Generate a customizable grant proposal template for environmental sustainability projects."*

4. Improving Budget Justifications for Transparency

✦ *"Rewrite this budget justification to ensure clarity, funder alignment, and a strong rationale for each expense."*

5. Enhancing Proposal Storytelling and Emotional Appeal

✦ *"Craft an engaging impact story for a grant proposal supporting first-generation college students."*

By leveraging **AI-powered best practices**, organizations can ensure their proposals **stand out and secure funding more consistently**.

Looking Ahead

Now that we've explored **real-world AI grant writing success stories**, the next chapter will focus on **how to future-proof AI-driven grant writing strategies**—helping organizations stay ahead of emerging funding trends and technological advancements.

Reflection Questions:

1. What lessons from these success stories can you apply to your organization's grant writing process?
2. How can AI be used to scale grant submissions without reducing proposal quality?
3. What AI-driven improvements can you make in your grant writing workflow to increase success rates?

Chapter 4, Section 4 Summary

✓ AI-powered grant writing has helped organizations secure millions in funding through increased efficiency and funder alignment.

✓ Key lessons include leveraging AI for proposal consistency, data-backed justifications, and budget transparency.

✓ AI improves funder-specific tailoring, enabling more competitive applications.

✓ By applying these insights, organizations can refine their AI-driven grant writing strategies for future success.

Chapter 5: Future-Proofing AI-Driven Grant Writing Strategies

Section 1: Emerging AI Trends and Innovations in Grant Writing

As AI technology continues to evolve, so do its **applications in grant writing and funding acquisition**. Organizations that **stay ahead of emerging AI trends** will be better equipped to **optimize workflows, increase grant success rates, and adapt to new funding opportunities**.

This section will explore:
- ✅ **Key emerging AI trends in grant writing**
- ✅ **How new AI innovations are shaping the future of funding applications**
- ✅ **Potential risks and ethical considerations of next-generation AI**
- ✅ **Practical AI prompts for preparing for future AI developments**

Key Emerging AI Trends in Grant Writing

AI is transforming the grant writing landscape by introducing **automation, predictive analytics, and enhanced funder alignment**. The following trends highlight **how AI will continue to shape funding strategies** in the years ahead:

Emerging AI Trend	How It Impacts Grant Writing
1. AI-Powered Predictive Analytics for Grant Success	AI will analyze past applications to **predict which grants are most likely to be funded**.
2. AI-Driven Personalized Grant Matching	AI will **match organizations to the best funding opportunities** based on historical success rates.
3. Natural Language Processing (NLP) for Funder Alignment	AI will refine proposals **to match funder language, priorities, and past award trends**.
4. AI for Real-Time Compliance and Formatting Checks	AI will detect **non-compliance with submission guidelines before proposals are submitted**.
5. AI-Generated Impact Forecasting	AI will predict **long-term social and economic impacts of funded projects**, strengthening justifications.

By leveraging these **emerging trends**, organizations can **adapt their grant writing strategies to stay competitive**.

📌 **AI Prompt:** *"Analyze our past five grant proposals and predict which future grants we have the highest likelihood of winning based on funding trends."*

How AI Innovations Are Shaping the Future of Grant Applications

1. AI-Powered Funder Relationship Management

- ♦ AI will help organizations **track funder interactions, past awards, and renewal opportunities**.
- 📌 **AI Prompt:** *"Generate a funder relationship strategy based on past interactions and grant renewal cycles."*

---

2. Voice-to-Text AI for Grant Drafting

- ♦ AI-driven **speech recognition** will allow grant writers to **dictate proposals instead of typing**, improving efficiency.
- 📌 **AI Prompt:** *"Convert this recorded project summary into a structured grant proposal draft."*

---

3. AI-Generated Data Visualizations for Grant Proposals

- ♦ AI will create **interactive charts, infographics, and data reports** to **improve proposal presentation**.
- 📌 **AI Prompt:** *"Generate a data visualization summarizing the expected impact of this community development program."*

---

4. Blockchain-Integrated AI for Grant Transparency

- ♦ AI and **blockchain technology** will be used to **enhance transparency in fund allocation and reporting**.
- 📌 **AI Prompt:** *"Outline a grant reporting strategy using AI and blockchain to ensure financial transparency."*

---

5. AI-Powered Grant Writing Chatbots for Team Collaboration

- ♦ AI chatbots will assist grant teams by **answering questions, generating content, and providing real-time editing suggestions**.

✈ **AI Prompt:** *"Set up an AI-powered chatbot to help our grant writing team streamline proposal editing and compliance checking."*

Potential Risks and Ethical Considerations of Next-Generation AI

As AI technology advances, organizations must be mindful of **potential risks and ethical challenges**:

Potential Risk	Why It Matters	Mitigation Strategy
1. Over-Reliance on AI Decision-Making	AI should **assist** grant writers, not replace strategic thinking.	Ensure **human oversight** in AI-generated content.
2. AI-Generated Bias in Grant Proposals	AI may **reinforce existing biases in funding decisions**.	Review AI outputs for **inclusivity and fairness**.
3. Ethical AI Data Usage	AI tools process **sensitive financial and project data**.	Use **secure, ethical AI platforms** to protect data privacy.
4. Accuracy of AI Predictions	Predictive analytics may **incorrectly estimate funding success**.	Validate AI predictions with **human expertise and historical data**.
5. Plagiarism & Copyright Issues	AI-generated content may **unintentionally replicate existing text**.	Use **plagiarism detection tools** before submitting AI-assisted proposals.

By addressing these **risks proactively**, organizations can **use AI responsibly while maximizing its benefits**.

✈ **AI Prompt:** *"Analyze this AI-generated grant proposal for potential biases and suggest revisions to improve inclusivity."*

Practical AI Prompts for Preparing for Future AI Developments in Grant Writing

1. Leveraging Predictive Analytics for Grant Success

✒ *"Analyze past funding trends and predict which types of grant proposals will have the highest success rate next year."*

2. Automating Grant Writing Workflows with AI

✒ *"Create a fully AI-integrated workflow for streamlining grant research, writing, and submission."*

3. Ensuring Ethical AI Use in Future Grant Writing

✒ *"Develop a set of ethical guidelines for using AI in our grant writing process."*

4. Preparing for AI-Driven Proposal Personalization

✒ *"Customize this grant proposal to align with the language and priorities of [specific funder]."*

5. AI for Real-Time Proposal Compliance Checks

✒ *"Set up an AI tool to detect and correct formatting and compliance errors in grant applications before submission."*

By staying ahead of **AI-driven innovations**, organizations can **future-proof their grant writing strategies and maximize funding success**.

Looking Ahead

Now that we've explored **emerging AI trends in grant writing**, the next section will focus on **how to build an adaptive AI strategy for long-term funding success**—helping organizations refine and optimize AI use over time.

Reflection Questions:

1. How can your organization prepare for AI-powered predictive analytics in grant writing?
2. What ethical considerations should you address as AI tools become more advanced?
3. How can AI-driven funder relationship management improve your long-term funding strategy?

Chapter 5, Section 1 Summary

✓ AI-powered predictive analytics and personalization will shape the future of grant writing.
✓ Emerging AI trends include funder relationship management, speech-to-text drafting, and interactive data visualizations.
✓ Ethical AI use requires balancing automation with human decision-making.
✓ Organizations that adapt to AI innovations will gain a competitive advantage in securing funding.

Section 2: Building an Adaptive AI Strategy for Long-Term Grant Writing Success

To remain competitive in the **evolving grant writing landscape**, organizations must develop an **adaptive AI strategy** that enhances efficiency, improves proposal quality, and aligns with future funding trends. A well-planned **AI integration strategy** ensures that AI **remains a powerful tool rather than a temporary solution**.

This section will explore:
✓ **Key components of a long-term AI strategy for grant writing**
✓ **How to continuously refine AI use for grant applications**
✓ **AI-powered tools and frameworks for sustainable funding success**
✓ **Practical AI prompts for developing an adaptive AI strategy**

Key Components of a Long-Term AI Strategy for Grant Writing

An adaptive AI strategy requires **continuous learning, workflow refinement, and human oversight**. The following components help organizations **leverage AI sustainably while improving funding success rates**:

Component	Why It's Important	How to Implement
1. AI-Integrated Grant Writing Workflow	Ensures **consistent AI-assisted research, drafting, and editing**.	Establish an **AI-enhanced step-by-step grant development process**.
2. Data-Driven Funder Alignment	AI helps identify **funders most likely to award grants based on past trends**.	Use AI to analyze **historical funding patterns and grant reviewer preferences**.
3. Continuous AI Model Improvement	AI must be trained with **updated grant writing best practices**.	Regularly **refine AI-generated content using successful proposals**.
4. AI-Powered Grant Performance Analytics	Measures **success rates, trends, and improvement areas**.	Use AI to track **funding application outcomes and refine future submissions**.
5. Ethical & Responsible AI Use	Prevents **data misuse, plagiarism, and biased content**.	Establish **AI governance policies for grant writing ethics and security**.

By **integrating these components**, organizations can develop an **AI strategy that evolves with the funding landscape**.

📌 **AI Prompt:** *"Develop a sustainable AI grant writing strategy that integrates research, proposal drafting, compliance checks, and funder analysis."*

How to Continuously Refine AI Use for Grant Applications

To maximize AI's effectiveness, organizations should implement a **cyclical improvement model**:

Step 1: Evaluate AI Performance After Each Grant Submission

✅ Measure the **quality, clarity, and impact of AI-generated proposals**.
📌 **AI Prompt:** *"Analyze the effectiveness of our last three AI-assisted grant proposals and suggest refinements."*

Step 2: Update AI Training Data with New Funding Trends

✓ AI must stay current with **funder priorities, compliance rules, and sector trends**.
★ **AI Prompt:** *"Identify emerging trends in federal education grant funding and suggest adjustments to our proposal strategy."*

Step 3: Implement A/B Testing for AI-Generated Grant Proposals

✓ Compare multiple AI-generated drafts to **identify which approach yields the highest success rates**.
★ **AI Prompt:** *"Generate two different versions of an executive summary for a healthcare grant and compare their impact."*

Step 4: Enhance AI Personalization for Different Funders

✓ AI-generated proposals should be **tailored to specific funder preferences**.
★ **AI Prompt:** *"Customize this grant proposal to align with the language and priorities of the [specific foundation]."*

Step 5: Track AI-Driven Grant Success Metrics Over Time

✓ AI can identify **patterns in successful vs. rejected applications**, guiding improvements.
★ **AI Prompt:** *"Generate a report comparing the success rates of AI-assisted vs. traditional grant proposals in the past two years."*

AI-Powered Tools & Frameworks for Sustainable Grant Writing Success

AI Tool/Framework	Function	Best For
AI-Integrated Grant Calendars	Tracks **grant deadlines, submission progress, and renewal dates**.	Nonprofits, universities, and foundations managing multiple grants.
Funder Interest Matching AI	Predicts **which funders are most likely to support specific projects**.	Organizations seeking **targeted funding opportunities**.
AI-Generated Proposal Libraries	Saves and structures **previously successful AI-enhanced proposals**.	Teams looking to **reuse and optimize winning templates**.
Predictive Analytics for Grant Success	Uses **historical data to predict the likelihood of securing funding**.	Organizations wanting **data-driven insights on funder behavior**.
AI-Powered Editing & Compliance Assistants	Scans **grant proposals for readability, clarity, and compliance issues**.	Ensuring **error-free and funder-aligned grant submissions**.

By integrating **AI-driven frameworks**, organizations can **build a scalable, data-informed, and adaptive grant writing strategy**.

✦ **AI Prompt:** *"Develop an AI-powered workflow for automating grant writing, submission tracking, and funder alignment."*

Case Study: Implementing an Adaptive AI Grant Writing Strategy for a Nonprofit

◆ **Background:** A nonprofit specializing in **community health initiatives** wanted to develop a **long-term AI-powered grant writing strategy** to secure more consistent funding.

◆ **Challenges:**

- **AI-generated proposals needed refinement** to meet funder-specific criteria.
- The organization lacked **data-driven insights on why some grants were rejected**.
- They needed an **AI-assisted tracking system** for multiple funding applications.

- **How the Nonprofit Built an Adaptive AI Strategy:**
✓ **Created a Continuous AI Feedback Loop** – AI **analyzed past funding trends** and suggested refinements for future submissions.
✓ **Implemented a Funder Interest Matching AI** – AI recommended **the most aligned funding opportunities**.
✓ **Developed AI-Integrated Submission Tracking** – AI tracked **submission deadlines, reviewer feedback, and award outcomes**.

- **Outcome:**
The nonprofit **increased its grant approval rate by 45%** within two years by continuously improving AI-assisted proposals.

- **Key Takeaway:**
- An adaptive AI strategy ensures ongoing refinement, leading to more effective, funder-aligned grant applications.

✦ **AI Prompt:** *"Develop a strategic AI-powered grant writing improvement plan for an organization seeking long-term funding success."*

Practical AI Prompts for Developing an Adaptive AI Strategy

1. Creating an AI-Integrated Grant Writing Workflow

✦ *"Outline a step-by-step AI-enhanced workflow for researching, drafting, editing, and submitting grant proposals."*

2. Using AI to Improve Long-Term Grant Writing Success

✦ *"Generate a strategy for continuously improving AI-generated grant proposals based on past funding feedback."*

3. Tracking Grant Writing Performance Metrics

✦ *"Develop a report template for tracking grant success rates and proposal effectiveness over time."*

4. Refining AI Personalization for Funder Alignment

✦ *"Adjust this grant proposal to align more closely with [specific funder]'s mission and funding priorities."*

5. Ensuring Ethical & Responsible AI Use in Long-Term Strategy

📌 *"Develop ethical guidelines for AI-driven grant writing, balancing automation with human oversight."*

By implementing **a long-term AI strategy**, organizations can **future-proof their grant writing efforts, maximize efficiency, and increase funding success rates**.

Looking Ahead

Now that we've covered **how to build an adaptive AI strategy for grant writing success**, the next section will focus on **how to train grant writing teams to effectively use AI tools**—ensuring smooth adoption and long-term efficiency.

Reflection Questions:

1. What steps has your organization taken to continuously refine AI-generated grant proposals?
2. How can AI-driven analytics improve your grant writing strategy over time?
3. What AI-powered frameworks could help streamline your grant writing and submission process?

Chapter 5, Section 2 Summary

✅ A long-term AI strategy ensures sustainable, adaptive grant writing improvements.
✅ Continuous refinement of AI-generated proposals improves success rates.
✅ AI-powered frameworks enhance funder alignment, compliance, and data-driven decision-making.
✅ Tracking AI-driven grant performance enables organizations to optimize submissions over time.

Section 3: Training Your Team to Effectively Use AI for Grant Writing

As AI becomes an integral tool in grant writing, **organizations must train their teams to use AI effectively**. A well-trained team can leverage AI to **increase efficiency, improve proposal quality, and secure more funding opportunities**.

This section will explore:
- ✅ **Why AI training is essential for grant writing teams**
- ✅ **Key components of an AI grant writing training program**
- ✅ **How to integrate AI training into an organization's workflow**
- ✅ **Practical AI prompts for developing training materials**

Why AI Training is Essential for Grant Writing Teams

Many organizations adopt AI tools but fail to **maximize their benefits due to a lack of training**. Common challenges include:

Challenge	Why It's a Problem	How AI Training Helps
1. Lack of Familiarity with AI Tools	Teams may not know how to use AI for **grant research, writing, or compliance**.	AI training provides **step-by-step guidance on effective AI utilization**.
2. Misuse of AI-Generated Content	Over-reliance on AI may lead to **generic, repetitive, or non-compliant proposals**.	Training ensures teams **review and refine AI outputs for quality**.
3. Ethical and Data Privacy Concerns	AI tools can unintentionally **compromise sensitive grant information**.	Training covers **best practices for AI security and ethical use**.
4. Inconsistent AI Integration Across Teams	Some team members may **use AI differently or inefficiently**.	A standardized **AI training program ensures consistency**.
5. Resistance to AI Adoption	Staff may be hesitant to **incorporate AI into their workflows**.	AI training demonstrates **how AI simplifies tasks and improves results**.

By addressing these challenges, organizations can **increase AI adoption and maximize its impact on grant writing success**.

➤ **AI Prompt:** *"Develop an AI training program outline for a nonprofit grant writing team."*

Key Components of an AI Grant Writing Training Program

A structured AI training program ensures **all team members understand how to effectively integrate AI into their grant writing processes**.

Training Module	What It Covers	AI Tool Example
1. Introduction to AI for Grant Writing	Overview of **AI applications in funding research, proposal writing, and compliance**.	ChatGPT, Gemini AI, Grants.gov
2. AI-Powered Grant Research & Matching	How to use AI to **find relevant funding opportunities**.	Instrumentl, OpenGrants
3. AI-Assisted Proposal Drafting & Editing	Best practices for **drafting proposals with AI** while maintaining funder alignment.	Grammarly, Hemingway Editor, ChatGPT
4. AI for Budget Justifications & Financial Reporting	Using AI to **format and clarify financial narratives**.	Excel AI, QuickBooks AI
5. AI for Compliance, Formatting, and Submission	Ensuring AI-generated proposals **meet funder requirements**.	AI Formatting Assistants, ChatGPT Compliance Checks
6. Ethical Considerations & Data Privacy in AI Use	Protecting sensitive grant data while using AI tools responsibly.	Secure AI Platforms, Internal AI Guidelines
7. Real-World AI Grant Writing Case Studies	Learning from **successful AI-enhanced proposals**.	AI-Assisted Proposal Libraries

By implementing **a structured AI training program**, organizations can **ensure their teams are well-equipped to use AI effectively in grant writing**.

➤ **AI Prompt:** *"Create a detailed AI training curriculum for a grant writing team focusing on research, drafting, compliance, and ethics."*

How to Integrate AI Training into an Organization's Workflow

To ensure **successful AI adoption**, organizations should integrate AI training into their **ongoing professional development efforts**.

Step 1: Conduct an AI Knowledge Assessment

✓ Evaluate team members' **current AI knowledge and skill levels**.
📌 **AI Prompt:** *"Develop an AI skills assessment quiz for grant writing teams."*

Step 2: Provide Hands-On AI Training Workshops

✓ Offer **interactive training sessions** where staff practice using AI tools.
📌 **AI Prompt:** *"Create an AI workshop agenda covering grant research, drafting, and compliance checks."*

Step 3: Implement AI Mentorship & Peer Learning

✓ Assign **AI-proficient staff members as mentors** to guide others.
📌 **AI Prompt:** *"Develop a peer mentorship program for training staff on AI-enhanced grant writing."*

Step 4: Establish an AI Resource Hub for Continuous Learning

✓ Maintain **an internal repository** of AI guides, tutorials, and best practices.
📌 **AI Prompt:** *"Create an AI knowledge hub with guides, FAQs, and troubleshooting resources for grant writers."*

Step 5: Evaluate AI Training Effectiveness & Gather Feedback

✓ Continuously **assess AI training effectiveness** and adjust programs as needed.
📌 **AI Prompt:** *"Generate a post-training survey to evaluate AI adoption and effectiveness in grant writing."*

By following these **steps**, organizations can ensure their teams **stay updated on AI advancements and maximize AI's impact on grant writing success**.

Case Study: Implementing AI Training for a Grant Writing Team

♦ **Background:** A **large nonprofit** with multiple grant writers wanted to standardize AI use across its team to **increase funding efficiency and success rates**.

♦ **Challenges:**

- Some staff **were resistant to AI adoption** due to lack of familiarity.
- Different teams **used AI inconsistently**, leading to **inconsistent proposal quality**.
- The organization lacked **a structured AI training program**.

♦ **How They Built an AI Training Program:**

✓ **Developed an AI Training Curriculum** – Covered **grant research, proposal drafting, compliance, and ethics**.
✓ **Hosted Monthly AI Workshops** – Provided **hands-on practice with AI tools**.
✓ **Implemented AI Mentorship** – Experienced AI users guided other staff members.
✓ **Tracked AI Usage Metrics** – Measured how AI **impacted proposal efficiency and quality**.

♦ **Outcome:**
🎇 The nonprofit **increased its grant application output by 30%** and improved proposal alignment with funder priorities, leading to a **higher grant approval rate**.

♦ **Key Takeaway:**
♦ AI training programs ensure that teams use AI effectively, consistently, and ethically for grant writing success.

📌 **AI Prompt:** *"Create a structured training plan for onboarding new grant writers to AI tools and best practices."*

Practical AI Prompts for Training Your Grant Writing Team

1. Teaching AI-Powered Grant Research & Matching

📌 *"Develop a training guide on using AI to identify the best funding opportunities based on project goals."*

2. Training on AI-Assisted Proposal Drafting

📌 *"Create an interactive workshop that teaches grant writers how to refine AI-generated proposal drafts."*

3. Ensuring Ethical AI Use in Grant Writing

📌 *"Develop a compliance checklist for ensuring AI-generated proposals meet ethical and privacy standards."*

4. Improving AI Adoption Across Teams

📌 *"Design an AI mentoring program where experienced grant writers help new team members integrate AI tools."*

5. Evaluating AI Training Effectiveness

📌 *"Generate a feedback survey for grant writers to assess their confidence in using AI for funding applications."*

By incorporating **structured AI training**, organizations can **boost productivity, enhance proposal quality, and increase grant success rates**.

Looking Ahead

Now that we've covered **how to train teams to effectively use AI in grant writing**, the next section will focus on **how to measure AI's long-term impact on grant writing success**—ensuring organizations track and optimize AI use over time.

Reflection Questions:

1. How can your organization create a standardized AI training program for grant writers?
2. What steps can be taken to ensure ethical and responsible AI use in grant applications?
3. How can AI mentorship and peer learning improve AI adoption across teams?

Chapter 5, Section 3 Summary

✅ AI training is essential for maximizing AI's impact on grant writing efficiency and success.
✅ A structured AI training program ensures consistent, ethical, and effective AI use.
✅ Hands-on workshops, mentorship, and continuous learning improve AI adoption.
✅ Organizations that invest in AI training see increased funding success rates.

Section 4: Measuring AI's Long-Term Impact on Grant Writing Success

AI-powered grant writing is an **investment in efficiency and funding success**, but how can organizations measure its **true impact over time**? Tracking AI's effectiveness helps refine strategies, justify AI investments, and **maximize funding potential**.

This section will explore:
- ✅ **Key performance indicators (KPIs) for evaluating AI's impact**
- ✅ **How to track AI-driven improvements in grant writing efficiency**
- ✅ **AI tools and methods for analyzing funding success rates**
- ✅ **Practical AI prompts for assessing long-term AI performance**

Key Performance Indicators (KPIs) for Evaluating AI's Impact on Grant Writing

To measure AI's effectiveness, organizations should track **quantifiable metrics** that reflect **productivity, funding success, and proposal quality**.

KPI	What It Measures	Why It Matters
1. Grant Submission Rate	Number of grant applications submitted per quarter/year.	AI **streamlines drafting and research**, increasing submission capacity.
2. Grant Approval Rate	Percentage of submitted grants that receive funding.	AI improves **funder alignment, clarity, and compliance**, increasing success rates.
3. Proposal Completion Time	Average time spent drafting and finalizing a grant proposal.	AI reduces **manual writing time**, allowing faster turnaround.
4. Editing & Compliance Efficiency	Time spent revising AI-generated drafts for clarity and compliance.	AI minimizes **errors, ensuring funder guidelines are met**.
5. AI-Generated Proposal Effectiveness Score	Quality assessment based on readability, funder alignment, and storytelling.	AI assists with **engaging narratives, structured justifications, and impactful storytelling**.

By regularly tracking **these KPIs**, organizations can assess **how AI enhances grant writing processes and funding outcomes**.

✦ **AI Prompt:** *"Generate a KPI tracking dashboard for monitoring AI's impact on our grant writing success over the past year."*

How to Track AI-Driven Improvements in Grant Writing Efficiency

1. Compare Pre-AI vs. Post-AI Grant Writing Metrics

✓ Analyze how **submission rates, funding approvals, and turnaround times** have changed since adopting AI.
✦ **AI Prompt:** *"Compare our last 10 grant proposals—five written without AI and five AI-assisted—to identify efficiency improvements."*

---

2. Monitor Time Savings in Grant Proposal Development

✓ Track how much **AI reduces time spent on research, drafting, editing, and submission preparation**.
✦ **AI Prompt:** *"Calculate the average reduction in proposal writing time since integrating AI-powered drafting tools."*

---

3. Measure AI's Impact on Proposal Quality & Funder Alignment

✓ Assess how AI **enhances proposal clarity, persuasiveness, and compliance with funder priorities**.
✦ **AI Prompt:** *"Evaluate the readability and alignment of our AI-generated grant proposals against past funder feedback."*

---

4. Identify Trends in AI-Driven Grant Success Rates

✓ Track whether AI-generated proposals **secure more funding than non-AI proposals**.
✦ **AI Prompt:** *"Analyze our grant approval rates over the past two years and determine AI's role in funding success."*

---

5. Collect Qualitative Feedback from Grant Writers & Funders

✅ Gather insights on **how AI improves workflows, proposal quality, and overall experience**.

📌 **AI Prompt:** *"Generate a survey for our grant writing team to assess AI's effectiveness and areas for improvement."*

By implementing these tracking methods, organizations can **quantify AI's long-term value and refine AI-driven grant writing strategies for continuous success**.

AI Tools & Methods for Analyzing Funding Success Rates

AI Tool/Method	Function	Best For
Grant Success Rate Analytics AI	Compares **win rates of AI-assisted vs. traditional proposals.**	Evaluating AI's impact on **funding acquisition.**
AI-Powered Writing Assistants	Tracks **revisions, readability, and compliance** in AI-generated text.	Improving **proposal clarity and funder alignment.**
AI-Driven Funder Matching Tools	Identifies **which funders align best with an organization's projects.**	Increasing **funder engagement and proposal success.**
Predictive AI for Grant Outcomes	Uses past data to **predict the likelihood of proposal approval.**	Helping **prioritize high-success-rate applications.**
AI-Based Grant Writing Heatmaps	Highlights **which proposal sections are most effective** based on past approvals.	Optimizing **narrative structure and impact storytelling.**

By leveraging these **AI tools and analytical methods**, organizations can gain **data-driven insights to improve future funding applications**.

📌 **AI Prompt:** *"Develop an AI-generated grant success prediction model based on our past five years of applications."*

Case Study: Measuring AI's Long-Term Impact on Grant Writing for a University

♦ **Background:** A **large university research department** integrated AI into its grant writing process to **increase funding acquisition and streamline proposal development.**

◆ **Challenges:**

- The team **struggled with time-consuming proposal drafting and compliance checks**.
- They lacked **a system for tracking grant success rates and AI's effectiveness**.
- Funders provided **unclear feedback on why some proposals were rejected**.

◆ **How the University Measured AI's Impact:**
✓ **Tracked Proposal Completion Time:** AI **reduced drafting time by 40%**, enabling more submissions.
✓ **Monitored Grant Approval Rates:** AI-assisted proposals had a **15% higher approval rate** than manually written proposals.
✓ **Analyzed Reviewer Feedback with AI:** AI helped **identify common funder concerns** and improved future applications.

◆ **Outcome:**
🎉 The university **secured 30% more research funding** and developed a **data-driven AI optimization strategy** for future proposals.

◆ **Key Takeaway:**
◆ Regular AI performance tracking ensures continuous improvement, increased funding success, and optimized proposal strategies.

✦ **AI Prompt:** *"Create a performance review framework to measure AI's long-term impact on our university's grant writing efficiency and funding success."*

Practical AI Prompts for Assessing Long-Term AI Performance

1. Monitoring AI's Role in Grant Submission Efficiency

✦ *"Analyze how AI has reduced the time required for researching, drafting, and finalizing grant proposals over the past year."*

2. Measuring AI-Generated Proposal Success Rates

✦ *"Compare grant approval rates of AI-assisted proposals versus manually written proposals to assess AI's effectiveness."*

3. Tracking AI-Driven Fund Alignment & Proposal Customization

📌 *"Evaluate how well AI-generated proposals align with funder priorities compared to past applications."*

4. Identifying Areas for AI Improvement in Grant Writing

📌 *"Analyze feedback from grant reviewers and suggest AI-driven refinements to improve proposal effectiveness."*

5. Assessing AI's Impact on Proposal Readability & Persuasiveness

📌 *"Compare readability scores and storytelling quality in AI-generated versus human-written grant proposals."*

By using **AI-driven analysis**, organizations can continuously optimize **funding strategies and ensure AI remains a powerful grant writing tool**.

Looking Ahead

Now that we've covered **how to measure AI's long-term impact on grant writing success**, the final section of Chapter 5 will focus on **strategies for staying ahead in AI-driven grant writing**—helping organizations remain competitive in an evolving funding landscape.

Reflection Questions:

1. How has AI impacted your organization's grant submission rates and funding success?
2. What tracking methods could improve your AI-driven grant writing evaluation process?
3. How can AI analytics be used to refine future grant proposal strategies?

Chapter 5, Section 4 Summary

✅ Tracking AI's impact on grant writing success requires monitoring submission rates, approval rates, and efficiency improvements.
✅ AI-driven analytics tools help refine proposal strategies and improve funding alignment.
✅ Continuous evaluation ensures AI remains an effective, evolving tool in grant writing.
✅ Organizations that measure AI's impact can optimize their funding success over time.

Section 5: Strategies for Staying Ahead in AI-Driven Grant Writing

As AI continues to transform grant writing, organizations must adopt **proactive strategies** to remain competitive and leverage AI's full potential. Staying ahead means **continuously refining AI workflows, integrating new AI innovations, and adapting to changing funder expectations**.

This section will explore:
- ✅ How to continuously adapt to AI advancements in grant writing
- ✅ Best practices for long-term AI integration
- ✅ How to future-proof AI-enhanced grant writing processes
- ✅ Practical AI prompts for staying ahead in AI-driven grant writing

How to Continuously Adapt to AI Advancements in Grant Writing

To **maintain a competitive edge**, organizations must remain flexible and responsive to **new AI capabilities and funding trends**.

Strategy	Why It's Important	How to Implement It
1. Stay Informed About AI Innovations	AI tools evolve rapidly, impacting grant writing efficiency.	Subscribe to **AI and funding newsletters**, attend AI webinars, and join AI grant writing forums.
2. Regularly Update AI Models with New Data	AI works best when trained on **current funding trends and success patterns**.	Use AI-driven **trend analysis tools** to update strategies.
3. Experiment with Emerging AI Features	New AI capabilities (like **predictive analytics**) can optimize funding success.	Pilot **new AI grant writing tools** before full adoption.
4. Incorporate AI into Organizational Strategy	AI should be **integrated into long-term funding plans**.	Develop **an AI policy for research, writing, and compliance**.
5. Encourage a Culture of AI Learning	Teams that continuously **improve AI skills** outperform others in grant success.	Host **regular AI training workshops** and mentorship programs.

By proactively **adapting to AI trends**, organizations ensure **consistent improvements in funding outcomes**.

📌 **AI Prompt:** *"Generate a list of upcoming AI innovations that could enhance grant writing efficiency and funder alignment."*

Best Practices for Long-Term AI Integration in Grant Writing

AI should be viewed as **a long-term asset**, not just a short-term solution. Successful organizations follow these **best practices**:

1. Establish AI Governance & Oversight

✅ Assign a **team leader** to oversee **AI use, compliance, and effectiveness**.
📌 **AI Prompt:** *"Develop an AI governance framework for ethical and strategic AI use in grant writing."*

---

2. Use AI to Track Long-Term Funding Trends

✅ AI can analyze **multi-year funding patterns** to **predict future grant opportunities**.
📌 **AI Prompt:** *"Analyze funding trends over the past five years and predict the most promising grant opportunities for next year."*

---

3. Automate Routine Grant Writing Tasks to Focus on Strategy

✅ AI should handle **research, formatting, and editing** so grant writers can focus on **narrative strength and funder engagement**.
📌 **AI Prompt:** *"Create an automated AI workflow for grant research, proposal drafting, and compliance checks."*

---

4. Invest in AI-Powered Collaboration Tools

✅ AI can **streamline grant teamwork** by enabling **real-time editing, funder tracking, and proposal development**.
📌 **AI Prompt:** *"Identify AI collaboration tools that enhance teamwork in grant writing."*

---

5. Create an AI-Optimized Proposal Library

✓ Maintain a **repository of successful AI-assisted grant proposals** for reference and improvement.
✦ **AI Prompt:** *"Develop a system for organizing and tracking AI-generated grant proposals for long-term refinement."*

By implementing these **best practices**, organizations can **maximize AI's role in securing sustainable funding**.

How to Future-Proof AI-Enhanced Grant Writing Processes

The key to **staying ahead** in AI-driven grant writing is **future-proofing strategies to adapt to evolving AI capabilities and funder expectations**.

Future-Proofing Strategy	How It Strengthens AI-Driven Grant Writing
1. AI-Driven Competitive Analysis	AI can analyze **how competitors use grant funding** to improve strategies.
2. Funder Sentiment Analysis	AI can track **funding priorities and funder language trends** over time.
3. AI for Multi-Layered Grant Collaboration	AI will facilitate **cross-organization grant partnerships**.
4. AI-Powered Funder Engagement Optimization	AI will identify **optimal funder outreach strategies** based on past interactions.
5. Blockchain-Integrated AI for Grant Transparency	AI will track **fund allocation and impact reporting** using blockchain technology.

✦ **AI Prompt:** *"Develop a five-year roadmap for integrating AI-driven innovations into our grant writing strategy."*

Case Study: How a Nonprofit Future-Proofed Its AI-Driven Grant Writing

♦ **Background:** A nonprofit specializing in **STEM education funding** sought to develop a **long-term AI-driven grant writing strategy**.

♦ **Challenges:**

- The team **struggled to track evolving AI tools** and **integrate new features**.
- Proposal quality **varied across grant writers**, leading to **inconsistent funder alignment**.
- Funders required **long-term impact forecasting**, which the team struggled to generate.

♦ **Future-Proofing Strategies Implemented:**
✓ **AI-Powered Grant Research & Funder Matching** – AI continuously **updated funding databases**.
✓ **Automated Proposal Refinement System** – AI ensured **standardized, high-quality proposals**.
✓ **AI-Generated Long-Term Impact Forecasting** – AI used **predictive analytics** to estimate **student success rates**.

♦ **Outcome:**
🎯 The nonprofit **increased its funding by 50%** over three years and **created an AI-enhanced funding roadmap**.

♦ **Key Takeaway:**
♦ By future-proofing AI strategies, organizations can ensure continuous funding growth and competitive positioning.

📌 **AI Prompt:** *"Design a future-proofing strategy to ensure AI-driven grant writing remains effective over the next five years."*

Practical AI Prompts for Staying Ahead in AI-Driven Grant Writing

1. Tracking AI-Powered Funding Trends

📌 *"Generate a report on how AI is transforming the nonprofit funding landscape over the next five years."*

2. Preparing for AI's Future Role in Grant Collaboration

📌 *"Develop an AI-driven strategy for securing joint grant funding with partner organizations."*

3. Using AI to Predict Future Grant Success Rates

📌 *"Analyze past funding patterns and predict which types of grant proposals will have the highest success rates in the future."*

4. Ensuring Ethical AI-Driven Grant Writing Practices

📌 *"Create an ethical AI usage policy for our grant writing team to ensure transparency and fairness."*

5. Optimizing AI for Personalized Funder Engagement

📌 *"Develop a funder outreach strategy that uses AI to tailor grant applications based on funder priorities."*

By integrating **forward-thinking AI strategies**, organizations can **remain leaders in AI-driven grant writing and maximize their long-term funding success.**

Looking Ahead

This section concludes **Chapter 5** on **future-proofing AI-driven grant writing strategies**. Next, we will transition into **Chapter 6: Conclusion & Final Recommendations**—summarizing the key takeaways and providing actionable next steps for AI-enhanced grant writing success.

Reflection Questions:

1. How can your organization stay ahead in AI-driven grant writing and funding strategies?
2. What AI innovations could you integrate into your long-term grant writing workflow?
3. How can AI help you build stronger funder relationships and optimize future grant applications?

Chapter 5, Section 5 Summary

✓ Organizations must continuously adapt to AI advancements in grant writing to stay competitive.
✓ Best practices for AI integration include governance, funding trend analysis, and proposal optimization.
✓ Future-proofing AI-driven grant writing ensures long-term funding success and adaptability.
✓ By leveraging AI innovations, organizations can maintain a strategic edge in securing grants.

Chapter 6: Conclusion & Final Recommendations

The integration of AI into grant writing has revolutionized the way organizations **research funding opportunities, draft compelling proposals, and align applications with funder priorities**. By leveraging AI strategically, organizations can **increase efficiency, enhance proposal quality, and improve funding success rates**.

This chapter will:
- ✅ **Summarize the key insights from this book**
- ✅ **Highlight the most impactful AI-driven grant writing strategies**
- ✅ **Provide final recommendations for maximizing AI's potential**
- ✅ **Outline next steps for organizations looking to integrate AI effectively**

6.1 Key Takeaways from AI-Driven Grant Writing

1. AI Increases Grant Writing Efficiency

- ✅ AI reduces the **time spent on research, drafting, and editing** by automating repetitive tasks.
- ✅ AI-powered **grant matching tools help identify the best funding opportunities faster**.

📌 **AI Prompt:** *"Summarize the ways AI has reduced grant proposal development time in our organization."*

---

2. AI Enhances Proposal Quality & Funder Alignment

- ✅ AI improves **clarity, storytelling, and funder-specific customization**.
- ✅ AI ensures **compliance with funder guidelines, increasing approval chances**.

📌 **AI Prompt:** *"Analyze the funder alignment of our latest AI-generated grant proposal and suggest refinements."*

---

3. AI Helps Organizations Scale Grant Submissions

- ✅ AI **streamlines workflows**, allowing teams to **submit more proposals with fewer resources**.
- ✅ Organizations can **reuse and refine AI-enhanced templates**, improving long-term efficiency.

📌 **AI Prompt:** *"Generate a scalable AI-driven grant writing workflow for submitting multiple proposals efficiently."*

---

4. Ethical AI Use is Critical for Long-Term Success

✅ AI should be used responsibly, with **strong data security and privacy protections**.
✅ Ethical AI practices include **transparent disclosure of AI assistance and human oversight**.

📌 **AI Prompt:** *"Create an ethical AI usage policy for our grant writing team."*

---

5. AI-Driven Data Analytics Improve Future Funding Success

✅ AI helps organizations **track grant success rates, funder feedback, and submission trends**.
✅ AI-powered **predictive analytics can forecast which grants are most likely to be approved**.

📌 **AI Prompt:** *"Develop a grant success prediction model based on our historical funding data."*

6.2 Final Recommendations for Maximizing AI's Potential in Grant Writing

To **fully leverage AI for grant writing success**, organizations should adopt the following **best practices**:

Recommendation	Why It Matters	How to Implement It
1. Establish AI Training Programs	Ensures all team members **use AI effectively**.	Offer **workshops, peer mentoring, and AI tool demonstrations**.
2. Use AI for Ongoing Grant Research	AI can **track emerging funding trends** to find new opportunities.	Set up **AI alerts for new grant opportunities and funding cycles**.
3. Customize AI for Funder Preferences	Personalized proposals **increase success rates**.	Train AI to **align proposals with funder mission statements**.
4. Continuously Refine AI Workflows	Optimized AI use **improves efficiency and accuracy** over time.	Regularly **analyze AI-generated proposal effectiveness and adjust workflows**.
5. Maintain Ethical Oversight & Compliance	Prevents **bias, misinformation, and security risks**.	Implement **AI governance policies and regular compliance checks**.

✦ **AI Prompt:** *"Generate a long-term AI adoption strategy for maximizing funding success in our organization."*

6.3 Next Steps for Organizations Implementing AI in Grant Writing

If your organization is **ready to take AI-driven grant writing to the next level**, consider the following **actionable next steps**:

Step 1: Assess Current AI Readiness

✓ Evaluate how AI is currently used (if at all) in **grant research, writing, and submission processes**.
✦ **AI Prompt:** *"Conduct an AI readiness assessment to determine how AI can improve our grant writing process."*

Step 2: Select & Implement the Right AI Tools

✓ Identify AI-powered tools that **align with your grant writing needs**.
📌 **AI Prompt:** *"Compare top AI grant writing tools and recommend the best fit for our organization's needs."*

Step 3: Train Staff for AI-Enhanced Grant Writing

✓ Offer AI literacy workshops and **hands-on training to ensure smooth adoption**.
📌 **AI Prompt:** *"Develop an AI training program for our grant writing team, covering research, drafting, and compliance."*

Step 4: Establish AI Performance Tracking Metrics

✓ Monitor **AI's impact on submission rates, approval rates, and proposal quality**.
📌 **AI Prompt:** *"Set up a tracking dashboard to measure AI's impact on our grant writing success."*

Step 5: Continuously Optimize AI Grant Writing Workflows

✓ Regularly refine AI-generated proposals **based on funder feedback and performance analysis**.
📌 **AI Prompt:** *"Analyze past grant reviewer feedback and recommend AI-driven improvements for future proposals."*

6.4 Final Thoughts: The Future of AI in Grant Writing

The use of AI in grant writing is still evolving, and **organizations that embrace AI strategically will gain a competitive advantage** in securing funding. The **most successful grant-seeking organizations will be those that:**

✓ Balance AI automation with human creativity and oversight.
✓ Use AI for efficiency while ensuring ethical, personalized, and funder-aligned proposals.
✓ Stay informed about new AI advancements and funding trends.
✓ Continuously refine AI-driven grant writing strategies to maximize funding success.

📌 **AI Prompt:** *"Create a roadmap for integrating AI-driven innovations into our grant writing process over the next five years."*

Final Call to Action: Embracing AI for Grant Writing Success

AI is **not just a tool—it is a game-changer** in the grant writing process. By following the strategies outlined in this book, organizations can:

- 🚀 **Enhance efficiency** – Automate repetitive tasks and improve workflow.
- 🚀 **Increase funding success rates** – Align proposals with funder priorities.
- 🚀 **Scale grant applications** – Submit more high-quality proposals with less effort.
- 🚀 **Optimize funding strategies** – Use AI-driven insights to improve long-term outcomes.
- 🚀 **Ensure ethical AI use** – Maintain transparency, compliance, and human oversight.

Organizations that **adopt AI strategically and adapt to evolving funding landscapes will be well-positioned for long-term success**.

📌 **Final AI Prompt:** *"Develop an AI-powered funding strategy to increase our grant approval rates and long-term sustainability."*

Conclusion: The Future of AI in Grant Writing is Now

AI is **revolutionizing the grant writing process**, and the opportunities for funding success are limitless. Whether your organization is **just beginning its AI journey or refining an existing AI-driven strategy**, the future of grant writing **belongs to those who embrace innovation, continuously improve, and maximize AI's potential**.

Are You Ready to Transform Your Grant Writing with AI?

This book has provided **the tools, strategies, and insights needed to integrate AI effectively** into grant writing. Now, it's time to **take action and implement AI-driven approaches** to **secure more funding, streamline processes, and future-proof your organization's grant writing success**.

🚀 Start today—embrace AI, refine your grant writing strategy, and unlock new funding opportunities!

Final Reflection Questions

1. How will AI help your organization **scale its grant writing efforts and secure more funding?**
2. What are the **first steps** you will take to integrate AI into your grant writing process?
3. How can you ensure that AI is used **ethically, strategically, and effectively** for long-term funding success?

Chapter 6 Summary: AI-Powered Grant Writing Success

✅ **AI enhances efficiency, improves proposal quality, and increases funding success rates**.
✅ **Organizations must balance AI automation with human oversight for best results.**
✅ **Continuous AI refinement ensures sustained success in grant writing**.
✅ **The future of AI-driven grant writing is now—organizations must act to stay ahead**.

Appendix: Essential Resources for Grant Writers

A curated list of tools, platforms, and references to support grant writers in leveraging AI, improving proposal quality, and increasing funding success.

1. AI-Powered Tools for Grant Writing

AI-driven platforms to enhance research, drafting, and compliance.

Tool	Primary Function	Best Used For	Website
ChatGPT	AI-powered content generation	Drafting proposals, rewriting sections, brainstorming ideas	openai.com/chatgpt
Grammarly	AI-driven grammar and style checker	Proofreading, tone enhancement, clarity improvement	grammarly.com
Hemingway Editor	Readability improvement	Ensuring concise and impactful writing	hemingwayapp.com
Instrumentl	AI-powered grant research	Finding and tracking funding opportunities	instrumentl.com
Grants.gov AI	Federal grant search and submission tracking	Identifying and applying for government funding	grants.gov
Excel AI (Microsoft Copilot)	Budgeting and financial analysis	Structuring grant budgets, financial reporting	microsoft.com
Notion AI	AI-driven knowledge organization	Managing grant writing projects and collaboration	notion.so

2. Grant Research & Funder Matching Platforms

Find the best funding opportunities aligned with your organization's mission.

Platform	Function	Best Used For	Website
Foundation Directory Online	Searchable database of private and corporate foundations	Identifying funders for nonprofit projects	candid.org
GrantStation	Comprehensive grant funding database	Researching private, state, and federal grants	grantstation.com
Pivot-RP	AI-powered research funding database	Finding grants for academic and research institutions	exlibrisgroup.com
OpenGrants	AI-driven public and private grant search	Tracking emerging grant opportunities	opengrants.io
GrantWatch	Searchable database of current grants	Finding government and foundation grants	grantwatch.com

3. Proposal Writing & Budgeting Guides

📖 *Key resources to improve grant writing skills and budget structuring.*

Resource	What It Covers	Access
The Foundation Center's Guide to Proposal Writing	Best practices for structuring and submitting winning proposals	candid.org
Winning Grants Step by Step (Tori O'Neal-McElrath)	Step-by-step guide to writing competitive grant proposals	Amazon
The Only Grant-Writing Book You'll Ever Need (Ellen Karsh & Arlen Sue Fox)	Comprehensive grant writing strategies and real-world examples	Amazon
OMB Uniform Guidance (2 CFR 200)	Federal grant regulations and compliance requirements	ecfr.gov
QuickBooks for Nonprofits & Churches	Budgeting and financial management for grant-funded projects	quickbooks.intuit.com

4. Online Courses & Grant Writing Certifications

Sharpen your grant writing skills with expert-led training programs.

Program	Institution/Platform	What It Covers	Website
Grant Writing Certificate Program	The Grantsmanship Center	In-depth grant writing and fundraising strategies	tgci.com
Professional Grant Writing Course	University of Notre Dame	Proposal development, funding research, and compliance	notredameonline.com
Udemy Grant Writing for Beginners	Udemy	Basics of grant writing and nonprofit funding	udemy.com
LinkedIn Learning Grant Writing for Nonprofits	LinkedIn Learning	Writing, budgeting, and securing funding for nonprofits	linkedin.com
Grant Writing Basics Course	Coursera (University of Michigan)	Writing compelling proposals and securing funding	coursera.org

5. AI-Powered Writing & Compliance Tools

Ensure grant proposals are clear, compelling, and funder-compliant.

Tool	Function	Best Used For	Website
WriteSonic AI	AI-powered content generation	Drafting persuasive grant narratives	writesonic.com
ProWritingAid	AI-driven editing and style analysis	Ensuring clarity, readability, and engagement	prowritingaid.com
Zotero	Research citation and reference management	Organizing grant-related research and references	zotero.org
Plagiarism Checker (Grammarly, Turnitin)	Ensuring originality of grant proposals	Checking AI-generated content for duplication	grammarly.com
Tableau Public	AI-driven data visualization	Creating compelling data-driven grant proposals	tableau.com

6. Grant Writing Communities & Networks

Join professional networks to stay updated on funding trends and best practices.

Community	Focus	Website
The Grant Professionals Association (GPA)	Networking, training, and resources for grant writers	grantprofessionals.org
Association of Fundraising Professionals (AFP)	Fundraising and grant development resources	afpglobal.org
Nonprofit Happy Hour (Facebook Group)	Peer support and nonprofit funding advice	facebook.com
Reddit Grant Writing Community	Discussions on grant writing challenges and opportunities	reddit.com
LinkedIn Grant Writing Groups	Networking and AI-driven grant writing discussions	linkedin.com

Final Thoughts

AI is transforming grant writing, but success still depends on strategic thinking, strong storytelling, and funder alignment. These resources will help grant writers:

- ☑ Stay informed about funding opportunities
- ☑ Improve proposal clarity and effectiveness
- ☑ Leverage AI ethically and efficiently
- ☑ Build lasting relationships with funders

AI Prompt to Generate Custom Resource Lists:
"Create a list of AI-powered tools, online courses, and funding databases tailored for grant writers seeking to optimize their workflow."

About the Author: Anthony J. Fitzpatrick, Ed.D.

Anthony J. Fitzpatrick, Ed.D. is an esteemed education leader, grant strategist, and expert in securing competitive funding to drive transformative change in schools and communities. With an exceptional track record in grant acquisition, Dr. Fitzpatrick successfully **secured over $3 million in competitive grant funding in a single year**, bringing critical resources to educational institutions through strategic, high-impact proposals.

As a **seasoned grant writer and educational administrator**, Dr. Fitzpatrick has successfully written and secured funding for **highly competitive grants**, including:

- ☑ **BiPartisan Safer Communities Stronger Connections Grant** – Advancing school safety initiatives and mental health supports.
- ☑ **Preschool Expansion Grant** – Increasing access to early childhood education opportunities.
- ☑ **Teacher Climate and Culture Innovation Grant** – Enhancing professional learning, educator retention, and workplace culture.
- ☑ **AI Innovation in Education Grant** – Integrating artificial intelligence into instructional practices and learning environments.

In his role as an Assistant Superintendent of Curriculum and Instruction, Dr. Fitzpatrick has overseen federal, state, and private grant portfolios, managing funding sources such as ESSER I, II, III, Perkins IV, ARP-HCY, and ESEA. His deep knowledge of grant compliance, program implementation, and strategic funder engagement has enabled schools to access millions in funding to support student learning, educator development, and school innovation.

Previously, as Director of School Innovation for the New Jersey Department of Education, Dr. Fitzpatrick led statewide education initiatives, ensuring that schools leveraged federal and state grant opportunities to implement research-based, sustainable improvements. His leadership in programs such as Future Ready NJ, Title IV funding, and competitive grant awards has empowered districts to modernize instruction, adopt cutting-edge technology, and improve student outcomes.

A thought leader in AI-driven grant writing, Dr. Fitzpatrick combines traditional funding expertise with emerging artificial intelligence strategies to help organizations streamline grant development, increase success rates, and scale impact efficiently. Through this book, AI-Powered Grant Writing: The Ultimate Guide to Securing More Funding with Artificial Intelligence, he provides actionable strategies, real-world case studies, and AI-powered insights to help grant writers maximize their funding potential in an evolving digital landscape.

www.ingramcontent.com/pod-product-compliance
Lightning Source LLC
Chambersburg PA
CBHW061812290426
44110CB00026B/2855